FENCING TO WIN

FENCING TO WIN

**Professor A.T. Simmonds
and E. D. Morton**

• THE •
SPORTSMAN'S
PRESS
LONDON

Published by The Sportsman's Press 1994

A catalogue record for this book
is available from the British Library

ISBN 0–948253–69–X

Printed in Great Britain by
Redwood Books Ltd, Trowbridge, Wiltshire

CONTENTS

LIST OF PLATES

ACKNOWLEDGEMENTS

Our sincere thanks are due to the following: Mr M. Fare, editor of *The Sword* and Mr G. Morrison of the A.F.A., for so kindly providing from their collections photographs for reproduction; Mr A. Ladd, who gave his services in an honorary capacity as our own photographer; Dr G. Foster, Mr E. Kelman, B.A.F., Mr D. Yu, and the other fencers of the London Hospital, Bromley and Gravesham Fencing Clubs who appear in the illustrations.

INTRODUCTION

The success of our previous work *Start Fencing* has encouraged us to embark on the present volume, aimed at those advanced fencers who are currently engaged, or hope soon to be engaged, in the more important competitions in their own countries and abroad. From the earlier book certain advanced strokes were deliberately excluded; the present one is not to be regarded as a sequel, for our new readers must not only be familiar with the whole theory and terminology of the game, but ought to be capable of executing any standard stroke with at least reasonable efficiency.

On the other hand, it does no harm to remind even the most advanced fencer of neglected truths or matters which he may know well enough, but which have drifted to the back of his mind. Brought back to his attention, they can have a stimulating effect on his game.

We have included sections on all three weapons, but as before, have endeavoured to combine the maximum of the classical technique without which no fencer can hope to be successful, or indeed to derive much pleasure from the sport, with the sternly realistic demands of modern competitions.

The emphasis throughout has been largely tactical, but separate tactical sections have been included for all three weapons, dealing with specific situations or special types of opponent. Epéeists and *sabreurs* should at least glance at the section on foil tactics and vice versa for foilists. Some comments are common to all weapons; others may repay study and stimulate the imagination.

It may be objected that in some cases we have decried the value of certain strokes in the fiercely competitive bouts of the present day, while in subsequent passages we have proffered advice on when and how to execute them. Any such inconsistency, however, is apparent rather than real; for every stroke in fencing is a possibility, given the right conditions, although the opportunities for some will be few and far between. It must, in the end, be the fencer and the fencer alone, with his opponent at sword-point, who decides what can and cannot be done with a reasonable chance of success in any given situation.

The technique of all weapons whether in their electric or non-electric form is, or should be, the same; this applies equally to the more recently electrified sabre. The electrification of this weapon has resulted in some changes, as was the case when the foil was first electrified, but we hope that in due course it will revert to its own natural course of development.

To save endless repetition of 'he or she', 'him or her', 'his or hers', we have used the masculine form of the generalised third personal pronoun.

Part One
BASICS

The basics ought not to be ignored by even the most advanced fencers. Often there can be some modification, adaption, or neglected truth which repays attention. Generally, the basics are common to all three weapons. Where some differentiation is necessary or advantageous, it will be noted.

The instructions throughout apply to the right-handed fencer, whom the left-hander must regard as his 'mirror-image', unless otherwise stated.

1: The Grip

Most coaches seem to encourage the use of orthopaedic grips even for eleven-year-olds, on the grounds, rightly enough, that added strength is given. Unfortunately, this renders difficult the use of certain parries – *prime* and lifted *quinte*, for example, let alone the circular parries. Youngsters who are encouraged, even pressurised, into using orthopaedic grips, may find it difficult, when older, to acquire the necessary technique, even if they are able or even prepared to devote the necessary time to practising. The essential wrist action should be supplemented by finger-play; it is regrettable that due to lack of early training, very few modern fencers are able to use their fingers at all.

Regarding the position of the thumb at foil and *épée*, there must be no argument. It must be placed definitely on top of the grip, with none of that lateral curve of the blade in mid-air produced by a slight degree of supination. A tendency in some quarters to advocate complete supination of the sword-hand is, in our opinion, totally inadmissible.

This applies equally to the *épée*. For the sabre, however, its own orthodox grip is vital. The ball of the thumb is on top of the handle; directly underneath it is the centre section of the forefinger on which the under-surface of the handle rests; the top section of the forefinger rests on the inner surface of the handle. As for the last three fingers, the under-surface of the handle must also rest on their centre sections, while their top sections are placed lightly on the handle's inner face.

It is absolutely essential that the grip should in no way resemble that of the French foil grip, with the handle in line with the thumb. On the contrary, the last fingers, by gripping, should bring the handle into a position almost at right-angles to the palm of the hand, and touching the point where the fingers join the palm. The fingers should manipulate the weapon with as much dexterity as at foil – the higher the degree of efficiency, the more delicate the hit. The majority of *sabreurs* will not, or at any rate have not, learned finger play, which accounts for their hard hitting.

We must apologise for dealing at such length with a matter which should be perfectly familiar to all intermediates, let alone anyone professing to be an advanced fencer; but there has been a recent tendency, among the coaches in certain areas, to permit a sabre grip which necessitates the delivery of cuts from the elbow, instead of by wrist and fingers.

2: On Guard

Suggestions have often been heard that the fencer should be 'more on his toes' than in the pre-electric days. This is dangerous doctrine. Body-balance, always relevant to each individual, is all-important; and here we can do no better than quote the words of Roger Crosnier in *Fencing with the Electric Foil*: 'We will ask the pupil to bear his weight on the balls of his feet, warning him not to go to the extreme of being on his toes'. For those who cannot learn to control their bodies, a slightly straighter knee position is now allowable, but this too must not be exaggerated. It should go without saying, but probably does not, that the weight should be evenly placed on each leg.

At *épée* the distance between the feet may be somewhat shorter than at foil; the leading foot thus gaining protection.

Due to the fact that the *flèche* is even more prevalent than at the other two weapons, many épéeists stand rather more upright, though at the price of sacrificing a certain amount of power. The *sabreur*, however, must adopt a more pronounced bend of the knees which promotes the sense of confidence, aggression, balance and above all, the power which is so essential at this weapon.

The feet are traditionally at right-angles and should probably remain so. For épéeists, the rear foot turned slightly forward will help body balance and relieve certain muscles. At all weapons, the front foot should be in line with the opponent's front foot. 'Toe to toe' is the watchword here.

There has been much alteration in the position of the trunk over the years. In quite early times there was a marked backward slope. In the classical era of 'steam foil', it was supposed to be perfectly upright. Certain masters of the new school in the early days of electric foil encouraged a very pronounced forward bend; all in all, a slightly forward inclination seems most appropriate to today's conditions. The same is true at *épée*, but at sabre the trunk should be distinctly upright so that the body-weight is dead even.

Volumes have been written about the chest, and whether it should be effaced altogether as was once fashionable in the Italian school, or whether, for the sake of comfort and easy movement, it should be half-turned to the line of attack. The effaced position obviously has a great theoretical advantage, and should be adopted as far as is possible in relation to the fencer's physique – always bearing in mind that it imposes much greater strain on the upper sword-arm. The position of the hips at sabre is more important than at any other weapon.

Despite what some modern masters say and a great many modern fencers do, the rear arm ought certainly to be maintained in its traditional raised position at both foil and *épée*.

The unarmed hand of the *sabreur* should be placed on his hip, fingers forward, thumb to the rear. Both arms being joined by the same set of muscles, the rear arm gives control, impetus and direction when efficiently used in the attack. And, yes, at sabre also, the rear arm is lowered; otherwise, it contracts the muscles above the left hip and inhibits the lunge.

As for the head, the same rule holds good as at all games. It should be perfectly still, moving only with the body. The line of vision should be eye to eye, not eye to blade.

The foilist's sword-arm should be in the classic position, but with the point of the weapon breast-high, not, as formerly, on the opponent's eye level. A great deal has been said about the advantages of a low-line guard, with absence of blade in *octave*. Very well, if that is what the fencer wants; but he should remember that he is vulnerable in the high line.

The position of the sword-arm is affected by the different weapons. It is generally agreed that the hand of the épéeist should be breast-high, as at foil, but some have been known to advocate holding it somewhat higher. This obviously exposes the underside of the forearm. Opinion is also divided on the extent to which the sword-arm should be extended. Three-quarters extended would seem to be favoured by current *épée* tactics.

Certain extremists formerly upheld the straight-arm guard. From shoulder to the point there was no deviation from a straight line. Several advantages accrued: the position gave every opportunity for a stop-hit; the *coquille* gave added protection when making counter-attacks; and it was easier to effect *dérobements* by means of multiple blade actions. Although for the normal opposition parry it was only necessary to raise or lower the point without bending the arm, there was a clear weakness in defence on the debit side. However, we are certainly of the opinion that in all cases the blade should be directed diagonally across the target at the opponent's forearm.

There used to be much debate about what exactly constituted the so-called 'offensive-defensive' position at sabre. Some advocated the blade being directed diagonally upwards across the opponent's target; others, a more vertical position. We approve the diagonal blade, with the hand level with the hip; but in our view, the best position when on guard is *seconde*, with the hand breast-high and the point directed at the opponent's front knee.

3: Footwork

1   The **step-forward** should be about the normal pace, that is, not more than about six inches. It must in any case be constant – otherwise the fencer confuses himself rather than his opponent. The error of bringing the rear foot closer to the front foot without realising it is all too prevalent even among internationals and must be eschewed. At sabre especially, steps should be short, fast and well-controlled, with the body-balance the same at all times. This can be acquired by controlled breathing and keeping the head still while the body is in motion. The movements of the head are a common cause of missed hits. The idea of 'braking', i.e., digging the toes into the *piste* to come to a sudden halt when threatened during an advance, or to change direction when retiring, is to be discouraged. It means a sudden change of body-weight and will take longer to reach maximum efficiency for the next action.

2   The **step-back** should be the same distance as the step forward and just as regular and consistent.

3   The **appel**   The tapping of the ground with the front foot serves no useful purpose whatever. It was supposed to 'unsettle' the opponent. If it ever did, he must have been of an unusually excitable or nervous disposition.

4   **Impetinata**   Not quite the same thing as the above, though some authorities have identified the two. The front foot is raised considerably higher off the ground with the toes cocked in the air; then the sole of the foot is brought down with the action of a horse pawing the ground. We seldom see it done, either because it is not taught or because fencers do not or will not practise it enough; but there is no doubt that it does speed up the lunge.

5 Balestra The object is to gain ground but not at the expense of a great unwieldy jump liable to throw the fencer off balance. The distanced covered should therefore not be more than the length of one's foot. It is perilous to use it at *épée*; too much opportunity is afforded for a counter-attack. It is most effective at sabre because of the power it engenders. The *balestra* is not used enough by British fencers, much practice being needed to ensure that a constant distance is gained. It is one way of achieving maximum speed with the *flèche*.

6 The Jump-back Lukovitch favours a 'scissors' action, with the leading leg passing behind the rear leg in the course of the movement. There is no real objection to this, though the similar technique whereby the leading heel kicks the rear heel, is quicker. The speed of reaction time is far quicker today than it was fifty years ago, so do not waste a period of fencing time shifting the weight about from one leg to another. Jump back from the lunge, or whatever, in any way that you like, provided that body-balance is maintained and that you are able to launch a riposte or counter-attack.

7 Side-steps should only be used tactically – in particular in defence against the left-hander.

8 In quartata and **passata sotto**, splendidly flashy actions, are, alas, impracticable, and in any case illegal nowadays.

4: The Lunge

The great majority of fencers, at the highest level, allow their rear foot to roll over in the lunge. This is still a mistake; no matter what they say, any secondary movements are severely handicapped. Sliding the rear foot along the *piste* instead of maintaining it rigidly in one position is, however, a different matter and a quite legitimate tactic when the lunge is started out of distance. If the front foot then over-lunges, the back foot may be allowed to drag to gain a vital extra three inches or so. But it is impermissible when lunging from the normal distance. A sliding lunge then will result in the fencer being too near his opponent to have any real hope of continuing the phrase or parrying a riposte. The sabre lunge often consists of little more than a large step and a pronounced drag of the back foot, which is to be condemned from the academic viewpoint. Ideally, the sabre lunge should be shorter than at foil, in order to recover to guard either forward or backwards, or to introduce any other foot action, as quickly as possible.

When the lunge is complete, the front foot should point straight ahead and the front knee and upper thigh should form a right-angle to the floor. The rear foot – we repeat this – should be flat, to facilitate any further actions, including recoveries forwards and backwards.

The normal recovery backwards is far easier if the feet are properly placed as recommended. These considerations apply equally to *épée* and *sabre*, though fencers generally ignore them.

Both arms form part of a complex set of muscles joined across the top of the back. If both arms are extended simultaneously, one to the front, one to the rear, so that they are horizontal as the leading foot is raised from the ground, speed and direction are gained and the hit should arrive before (or certainly not after) the foot reaches the floor. The rear arm of course finishes parallel with the rear leg, palm outwards. The classical masters used to say that the arm should not be swung away until half or even three-quarters of the way through the lunge. But with the above method, it stays in a more correct line. All this applies equally to épéeists, who would derive advantage from employing it.

Naturally, the *sabreur's* rear arm travels a shorter distance. The only other difference is that at the conclusion of the lunge the trunk is more upright, not inclined slightly forward.

When the foilist's sword-arm is extended with point in line, the weapon, hand and arm should be parallel to the ground. The hand should not be in the slightly raised position above the shoulder, formerly regarded as essential. The hand and arm must not be lowered during the lunge; it is the body which will carry the sword-arm down.

At sabre and *épée* the position of the blade of course varies according to the part of the target being threatened; but the sword-hand, with rare exceptions, should always remain breast-high and in line with the shoulder.

'Gaining on the lunge', by which we mean advancing the rear foot to touch the leading heel the instant before the front foot moves into the lunge, may have some tactical value; but too many fencers are guilty of an unconscious and partial imitation, which deprives them of the tactical advantage they might have gained if the action had been performed with technical correctness.

Latterly, we have begun to hear about the most mysterious varieties of the lunge: the 'explosive', the 'accelerated', the 'waiting'. Proper use of the rear arm helps the acceleration anyway; and how can one 'wait' in mid-air to 'discover' the parry? The thing is impossible.

There are only two ways to lunge – good and bad.

PLATE 1   FOIL: *en garde* (above) and the lunge (below)

PLATE 2   FOIL:

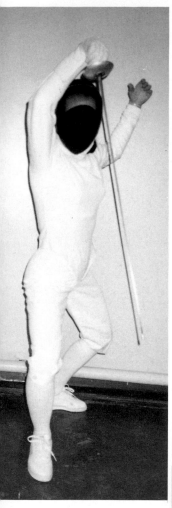

high *prime*

quarte

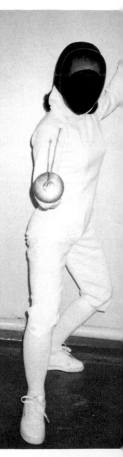

sixte

5: The Reprise

The old-fashioned lunge-recover-lunge combination is now too slow, even at foil. The renewed attack can be executed *en flèche* and has been found to be highly effective, more especially at *épée* and sabre. Better still is the execution of the *flèche* from the lunging position. (See below).

6: The *Flèche*

The *Flèche* is used more at *épée* and sabre than at foil. With the latter weapon it should not be employed unless success is virtually guaranteed. In sabre competitions there are far more *flèches* than other ways of reaching the target.

The first action is to extend both arms horizontally (as when lunging) and simultaneously to allow the body-weight to be displaced as far as possible over the front knee.

At the same instant, the rear knee is brought through, the foot landing on the heel and pointing, as nearly as possible, to the opponent. The fencer should run past his opponent with short, rapid strides. Vital points to remember are:

1   The hit should accompany the grounding of the rear foot – not a moment later.

2   The head must be kept still. The fencer should look above his opponent's mask, roughly about the height of a hand.

To *flèche* from the lunge position there are two methods:

1   Bring up the rear foot to the normal guard position (or even further), resting the ball of the foot on the ground without its being entirely flat. Then swing the rear leg through in the normal way.

2   Throw the body-weight right forward – this requires considerable strength in the front leg – then swing the rear leg through.

The method of the Hungarian masters, Lukovitch and Vass, is extraordinary. It involves swinging the front foot backwards to a point very close to the rear foot, which itself is advanced with an *appel* (Vass) alleged to accelerate the *flèche*.

Only a species of trained acrobat – certainly no fencer of our acquaintance – could hope to achieve anything like this. Few British masters could teach it and fewer British fencers would be prepared to study it.

7: The Fencing Measure

This is still lunging distance, that is, at foil, trunk to trunk. What follows may be slightly less applicable to épée and sabre where the distance is forearm to forearm.

Nevertheless, the measure has been increased at all three weapons because most fencers are uncertain of their ability to cope with the predominant absence of blade.

Preparations are therefore further apart, and despite the habit of closing the distance to finish the hit at close quarters, the attacker can still find himself out of distance without realising it and when he lunges cannot understand why he has been so easily parried.

Some fencers seem to have picked up a certain amount of Hungarian terminology – short, middle, long distance and the like – with which they only confuse themselves. Middle distance, to a British fencer, tends to mean riposting distance, though that is not the Hungarian interpretation. We prefer to adhere to the familiar classifications:

1   **Riposting distance**: when one can hit the opponent from the on guard position without any footwork.

2   **Lunging distance**: when a full lunge is needed to hit the opponent.

3   **Out of distance**: when a flèche or at least one step in addition to the lunge is needed to reach the opponent's target.

All distances are relative to the fencing measure, which itself varies for each fencer.

8: The Hit

The whole point of the foil or épée must arrive full-faced on the target, with no tendency to skid off. The electric weapon will not register unless the impact of the head is frontal. For this reason, the sword-arm must be parallel to the ground. (See *Lunge*). Moreover, the hit will arrive earlier.

The so-called 'flick hit', a highly angulated striking action with the point, is at present achieving much success, largely due to its novelty and to the fact that fencers are unused to defending themselves against it. Once they have become accustomed to doing so, its effectiveness will be reduced. These unorthodox methods have the disadvantage of withdrawing the point from the target.

The true art of a good hit at either foil or *épée* is the fact that the point is delivered directly towards the target.

At sabre the target is three dimensional.

Point attacks with the sabre are much the same as at foil and *épée*. The blade must be angulated inwards with the hand in pronation, chest high, receiving the full protection of the guard.

The whole of the fore-edge and the top third of the back edge can be used to deliver a cut. While making cuts to the various parts of the body, the height of the hand is regulated by both the riposte and the necessity of protecting it. Full use must be made of the *coquille* for the defence of the hand.

We insist that the cut should be delivered with the use of the fingers, and the fingers alone, the little finger supplementing the manipulators. The elbow should in no way be used to deliver the hit although a slight flexing of the wrist can be used to supplement the finger-play.

Part Two
THE FOIL

1: Attacks

It may seem to be stating the obvious to say that the object of any attack is to score a hit. Yet you score a hit, not because you are a good fencer, but because the opponent has made a mistake. No one attack is more successful than another – all depends on the opponent. Sometimes a straight thrust is all that is needed, at others a one-two or *doublé* is required. Therefore, all attacks must be related to the opponent's tactics, cadence and technique. Distance, time, cadence, are the essential factors in an attack. As a premise, it may be said that the best time to attack is on the opponent's step forward. In any case the attack should arrive on the target before the leading foot is grounded.

All attacks can be executed with or after the making or breaking of ground; when immobile, or with mobility (*en marchant*); progressively, or with broken time; or 'defensively', i.e., from the guard position.

It is important to remember that when lunging, an attacker should breathe out; on the recovery, he should breathe in. More will be said of this later.

A competent modern foilist should be able to execute a straight thrust on:

1 absence of blade
2 an engagement
3 a change of engagement
4 with or without a step forward.

He must also be able to disengage and cut-over from the high and low lines from:

1 engagement
2 change of engagement
3 beat
4 the above with a step forward
5 following a step forward with engagement.

Much has been written in the past on the exact technique of the disengagement and counter-disengagement, whether the former should be V- or

U-shaped, and whether the latter should be huge, or, as the old masters used to say, 'the size of a sixpence'. The truth is that all fencing is governed by straight lines and circles – the straight line to hit, the circle to deceive the blade. The size of the circle depends entirely on the part of the target that the attack is intending to hit.

The disengagement from a *quarte* engagement or relationship of the blades should go over the opponent's sword-arm. When disengaging from *sixte*, the blade may go to the lower part of the target. The disengagement is less applicable in the low line, but when executed, it can finish in the opposite low line or on the higher part of the target, or even angulated to the opponent's back.

When starting out of distance, blade contact may be made during the step. The disengagement itself may coincide with the grounding of the rear foot, or even after the lunge has started.

Against an engagement with strong opposition, the attacker will find that a disengagement with equally strong opposition by himself is an effective answer.

The cut-over may be similarly employed following an engagement, going diagonally across the opponent's body from the high line to the low line.

Nevertheless, a simple blade action will seldom be successful. However, to be paradoxical, we may say that all attacks are simple – but not simple. It certainly cannot be denied that the last action of any compound attack must be simple; and all depends on the last action in the line in which the hit is delivered. Compound, no less than simple actions, must be progressive and gain as much time and distance as possible. Today's attacks are almost invariably compound and complex, covering time and distance. The more the distance is opened up, the more complex they become. Like any attack, to be successful they must anticipate the parry. The old idea of a distinct feint drawing a distinct parry is now far too slow. The opponent must be studied and preparations, including feints, or rather indications of feints, must disguise the final attack.

Just as at sabre, many foilists are now reluctant to react to a feint; they hold back and hope to parry *en finale*. Therefore they must be rendered uncertain about the final line of the attack and so not know where to parry. Therefore the parts of the target threatened during a flowing, progressive attack ought ideally to be spaced widely apart – in other words, the old idea of, say, a one-two keeping as close as possible to the opponent's blade is now totally outmoded.

Nevertheless, the more a reaction can be provoked, the better. An unexpected, quick start sometimes causes a defensive reflex; so occasionally, can a *passé* feint, e.g., a beat or engagement without any semblance of a thrust. A shorter feint, with reduced depth and period of arm extension may upset a very nervy fencer. Against the controlled, steady fencer, a longer, deeper feint is needed, so the attacker must be able to round the former's blade very late in the lunge.

One beautiful and classical action is still highly effective – the *coupé-dessous*. The hand may be pronated to facilitate the hit beneath the opponent's sword-arm. From a *quarte* position facing a left-hander, it must of course be supinated.

The *coupé-dessous* is in theory feasible against a left-hander from a start in *sixte*, and the finishing point on the target is again his *octave*.

Today's use of the *doublé* as an attacking action is limited because most fencers fail to realise that their opponents are taking circular parries either in the high or low line. Counter-disengage twice is surely the one for the opponent who whirls his blade round and round; or a counter-disengage-disengage if he tries a lateral parry. It is an unfortunate fact that, contrary to time-honoured opinion, very wide blade movements are much harder to deceive than small ones.

Because of today's absence of blade, the withdrawal of the sword-arm in the cut-over has a devastating effect and gives a wider scope for any type of second blade action. It can be executed both as a simple and compound attack (*coupé–coupé*); particularly during any step forward.

The *coulé*-disengage, executed with variations of the depth of the feint and co-ordination with the footwork, was a popular and highly successful stroke until fairly recently; nowadays, one would rarely provoke the necessary covering action.

The 'high-low' attack is too often neglected and the same may be said of the corresponding attack commencing in the low line. In the latter case immediately after passing the opponent's blade, the final attack may be delivered to the upper target, in strong preference to the lower area.

A diagonal attack high-low or vice versa obviously has the great advantage of finishing on that part of the target diametrically opposite to that which was initially threatened.

Crosnier's compound attacks (*Electric Foil*):

He lists the following:

Feint straight thrust, disengage.

Feint straight thrust, Counter-disengage

Feint straight thrust, Cut over

Each ending in high or low line.

If executed at the right moment, especially on the opponent's preparation, and in particular, his step forward, all these attacks stand an excellent chance of success.

2: Parries

At electric foil, defence is more important than offence; its essential function is to prepare the way for an effective riposte. All parries are equivalent to guards. They must be made at the most appropriate distance from the body.

Whether they are taken with the hand slightly forward or backward depends entirely on the opponent's distance, but in any case the hand must not be dropped. If the distance requires it, the parry can of course be accompanied with a step back. Sometimes devastating effects can be obtained by parrying with a step forward, but this requires great confidence.

All parries are equivalent to guards, and protect a line. Just as with the distance, the parry is related to the attack, e.g., a counter-parry should really only be taken when the blades are close. We do not agree with the 'wide circle' which has been recommended by some theorists. The position of the hand must be related to the coming riposte. Some modern fencers change their position all the time from *sixte* to *octave* and back again, with slightly wider movements than used to be the case; thus they can prepare the way for an attack, or, alternatively, fall back to a parry.

Gallons of ink have been spilt on the age-old controversy regarding the respective merit of parries by opposition and detachment. The former should be used against the opponent with a strong hand. It has also been urged that it allows a choice between a riposte with opposition or by detachment, although it must be remembered that ripostes, especially in the heat of competition, are largely instinctive. The opposition parry will usually delay the riposte, while the parry by detachment is instinctive, immediate, and has the advantage in time and distance.

It is perhaps obvious, but may be worth a mention, that while angulated attacks are not always deliberate, and in any case can hardly be foreseen, almost any fencer will instinctively apply greater width and strength in the parry against the additional force of the attacking blade.

The innumerable parries of olden days – Danet, in the eighteenth century, identified no less than eighteen simple parries alone – were steadily reduced as time wore on. After World War II, most masters taught four only – *quarte* and *sixte* in the high line, *septime* and *octave* below. Since then, fencing has become far more aggressive, more like what an actual duel might be, and the 'old' parries, *prime*, *seconde*, and *tierce*, have staged a comeback.

Prime can be executed with either a pronated or supinated hand. The latter method may be better suited to some fencers using an orthopaedic grip. You should be able to see your opponent through the angle formed by the foil and the arm, not over the top of the arm. *Prime*, like *quinte*, is an excellent defence against the *flèche*. It should not be used against the lunge, if your opponent is too low for it to be effective; *quarte*, or a bind into *octave* are far preferable.

Seconde or **tierce** can be used for added control against very strong low line attacks. It should be emphasised that the latter is not the 'high' *tierce* of the classical school which was virtually the same as *sixte* with a pronated hand; it is the equivalent of sabre's low *tierce*, with the hand close to, and about level with, the leading thigh. In *seconde*, the point should be level with the opponent's leading knee.

From this position, the fencer must be prepared to parry *prime*, *quinte* or *sixte*, as the attack will almost certainly be delivered in the high line.

Quarte and **septime**. Do not direct the point out of line, as has been recommended in some quarters. It slows the riposte, losing time and distance. Nor can we endorse the view that *quarte* with the hand very low, blade almost vertical, can replace *septime*, except perhaps at very close quarters; still less that an exaggeratedly high *seconde* can form an acceptable alternative to *sixte*. In the high lines the point should be no higher than the opponent's throat.

Quinte. This is not the parry that once passed under this name and was later scathingly dismissed as a 'bad *quarte*'. The hand was low, pronated, and the point directed outwards, almost forty-five degrees across the adversary's blade. The modern parry is akin to the sabre *quinte*, that is, the hand is in line with the shoulder, head high, and the blade almost at right-angles beneath that of the opponent. It is an excellent example of a parry preparing a riposte. It may also be used as a preparation of attack.

Circular parries, partly because many attacks are launched wide of the blade, are too big these days, and if the opponent has been allowed to come a little too near, too often have the effect of dragging the point onto the target, whereas a parry which is correct in relation to the attack may well compensate for a slight misjudgment of distance.

There is more low-line fencing than in those halcyon days when the foil target terminated at the waist. Therefore, fencers must be well-versed in the half circular parries, and this does not merely mean from high to low, but vice versa. They should also practise the low circular parries, counters of *septime* and *octave*, for as Crosnier has observed, when fencing in the low line, it is dangerous to rely solely on the half-circular parries.

Most attacks nowadays are preceded by some form of footwork, thereby covering two periods of fencing time; but so aggressive are they that the blade action at the end is simple rather than compound, though that is what it was at the outset.

However, any combination of parries doubles one's protection, and is better than a single parry unless the attack is distinctly and unmistakably simple. Many parries are instinctive, but all are linked in pairs, diagonally, vertically and horizontally, e.g., *sixte–quarte, sixte–octave, sixte–septime* and so on. Ideally, all combinations can be taught to a sufficiently intelligent fencer.

It is not necessary always to step back with the first parry. All depends on the distance.

Ceding parries are essential to the repertoire and are particularly advocated against those who exert strong opposition. The arm and hand should travel back towards the body to adopt the best position for a riposte.

3: Ripostes

It has always been unwise to over elaborate at fencing and today this is truer than ever. The direct riposte may be described as 'the jewel in the crown' at both foil and *épée*. It is clearly the fastest and best controlled riposte, in which the fencer has complete control of all his faculties. Ideally, the riposter should be in the *en-garde* position and deliver the riposte with no movement whatsoever apart from the sword-arm; although there is a case for dipping the knees when riposting low.

As with parries, certain schools have at different times argued the case for ripostes with opposition of blades. Apart from the fact that these are none too easy to execute, the detached riposte stands alone for sheer speed.

When other conditions prevail, different answers must naturally be sought. The indirect riposte with opposition is very useful in deflecting the *remise*. The low disengagement to the small of the opponent's back should only be used against the left-handed fencer. Against a fellow right-handed fencer it should be left to the real experts who may also find it serviceable as an attack. From *quarte*, the riposte direct and, with the exceptions just mentioned, the ordinary disengagement riposte are the only really effective ones.

The riposte by straight thrust with strong opposition is more practicable after a parry of *sixte* than *quarte*. Alternatively, a disengagement from *sixte* may be made either into the high or low line. When riposting low, the hand should be pronated or supinated to suit the individual taste.

A successful parry of *septime* presents the joyous spectacle of a completely open target. Some writers have been at great pains to advertise the value of a 'lifted' *septime* – almost in fact, a *prise-de-fer* following the initial contact. It is permissible, but it confers no real advantage.

A direct riposte with opposition follows naturally from *octave*. It is of course possible to disengage high, but by the laws of nature this takes longer and time is precious. If, however, tactics demand this stroke, the wrist should be bent upwards, as indeed is the case when starting from *seconde*.

This brings us to **angulated ripostes** delivered downwards with an almost vertical blade. Many fencers fall forward at the end of the lunge, allowing their heads and trunk to drop, so that they are vulnerable on the back of the shoulder to such ripostes, particularly from *prime* and *seconde* when the legs should straighten. At foil, ripostes *en flèche* are purposeless. There is no point in staking everything on one stroke when the distance does not require it.

The riposte by cut-over   The parry and withdrawal of the arm from the elbow are virtually simultaneous. The point is brought down in line on the target with the utmost possible speed; another example of a stroke used long ago which has recently regained popularity and may fairly be attempted.

Compound Ripostes

To be successful, compound ripostes must be executed in the time that it takes to make an indirect riposte. Speed is of the essence and there should be no delay to wait for an opponent's reaction following the parry of his attack. His next move must be correctly predicted, preferably as the result of observation, or possibly as an inspired guess.

As compound means more than one blade action, we will use two disengagements as the example. Disengagements are really the only option, as circular parries on the lunge are impracticable. The attacker having been parried in *quarte*, closes his *quarte* line against a direct riposte. The defender feints a disengage and instantly, without losing time waiting for any reaction, makes the second disengage. If the opponent has tried to parry *sixte* to the feint, well and good. If he has not, the hit must be directed into the low line. It should not be necessary to stress that the sword-arm must not be straightened until the opposing blade has been cleared the second time; but there is always a danger of being carried away in the heat of the moment.

This stroke should not be attempted from *sixte* – one runs into the opposing blade if there is no second parry. Most people will parry simple; as stated above to attempt to take circular parries on the lunge is impracticable.

Counter-Ripostes

A counter-riposte on the lunge is still a possibility. When parrying the riposte, both point and hand should remain at the same relative height as when in the *en garde* position. The blade ought not be raised to the near vertical position which was sometimes taught in the past. The parry should itself be simple, and no counter-riposte on the lunge should ever be compound; and the question of when a counter-riposte should be delivered *en flèche* is entirely a matter of distance.

When the whole action has been premeditated, the hand may be only slightly withdrawn for the parry, so that the counter-riposte is almost instantaneous, and, executed with full opposition, might almost be classified as a sort of time hit on the riposte.

To strike home, with the counter-riposte, it may be necessary to recover to guard forward and go for the hit with a *reprise* action.

In such a case the parry may have to be taken while still on the lunge, or while recovering. A final blade action which is compound is more likely to harass the retreating fencer.

After a recovery backward, the counter-riposte from the *en garde* position can either be instinctive or premeditated, another example of second intention.

This leads to a consideration of the second counter-riposte. Nowadays the phrase leading to it is chiefly made *en marchant*, either forwards or backwards. Normally, both the counter-ripostes will be direct. All indirect actions will tend to slow things down. The first counter riposte and, more frequently the second, can be by *flèche*. For the sake of clarity:

A attacks with either a lunge or a step

B parries and ripostes

A parries and counter ripostes (first counter-riposte)

B parries and counter ripostes (second counter-riposte)

A may either recover to guard backward or forward after the parry of his attack or counter-riposte.

B will of course be either advancing or retiring correspondingly.

When playing for the second counter-riposte, the first riposte may allowably be a little short.

4: Counter-Attacks

The Stop-Hit

A stop-hit is an attack delivered on the opponent's attack or preparation of attack so that a period of fencing time is gained. In other words the stop-hit must arrive before the final action of the attack is commenced, e.g., a stop-hit on a step forward must arrive before the front foot moves forward into the lunge. We think it unnecessary to distinguish between the stop-hit from the classic on-guard position and the stop-hit with a lunge, which used to be classified as an 'attack on the preparation'. The principle of the timing is exactly the same, the sole distinction lies in distance.

The stop-hit should be reserved for use against the bent-arm attacker, the attack in two periods of fencing time and, above all, the step forward. It is highly unwise to venture the stop-hit against the great majority of attacks. Few nowadays are executed with one or more distinct feints, and even supposing the stop-hit arrived at all, it would almost certainly be declared invalid.

The reader is warned against attempting a stop-hit by disengagement. It is impracticable. Still less should there be any idea of disengaging on the opponent's attempt to engage. Modern fencers start out of distance and by the time anyone was near enough for any such action it would be too late. For anything more than a fifty per cent chance of success, the stop-hit must be direct.

The coaching books used to be full of examples of compound counter-attacks, but such things are virtually impossible today. Similarly, the idea of a stop-hit, parry and riposte in imitation of the sabre repertoire is only of value as a training technique.

The Time-Hit

For the advanced fencer, a time-hit is simply a stop-hit in a covered line. Therefore it may be successfully employed against the last stage of an attack, provided always that the oncoming blade is deflected; this is one reason why the time-hit is less efficient than the stop-hit proper – the latter arrives earlier in the proceedings, while it is difficult correctly to anticipate the opponent's final line.

Theoretically, there are as many time-hits as parries, though execution in some lines will obviously be extremely difficult.

Some writers, revelling in theory, have seen fit to distinguish between active and passive counter-attacks. The former, probably with a lunge, arrested the opponent's attack at the outset. The latter was delivered on the penultimate or even the ultimate phase of the attack. The cardinal issue as far as the stop-hit is concerned, is the gaining of fencing time. That once ensured, the exact moment or bodily position from which the counter-attack is launched is immaterial.

5: Preparations

Footwork

Vass and Lukovitch suggest in all seriousness that the cross-step backwards and forwards is an effective alternative to the normal step. Apart from the fact that it takes longer, it is a visual betrayal, and far more likely to alert the fencer to the fact that his opponent is on the advance.

We have said earlier that dancing about on the toes does no good at all. Body-balance is everything; any loss of balance will immediately put one at risk; so the fencer is advised to keep the soles of both feet flat on the ground. Either foot can then be lifted safely. But if on the tu. ; or even on the balls of the feet, lifting them at once impairs the balance.

With the quick step-forward-lunge, the arm should be straightened after the step, not before. This not only disguises the attack, but makes it easier to parry an attack on the preparation. But if more than one step is taken, the arm should be extended early, to establish right of way.

When a *balestra* precedes the attack, the fencer is again vulnerable and a parry may be needed. Therefore, as with the single step, the arm should not be extended until the jump is complete. There is no need to land with the weight on the rear foot to give additional impetus to the lunge; perfect balance is again what counts. If the step or *balestra* is followed by a *flèche*, the arm should be straightened before the forward inclination of the body, as this helps to initiate the attack.

A very famous master of long ago strongly recommended that the *balestra*, as opposed to a step, should always accompany a beat. While not entirely rejecting this, we still see little wrong with the step.

All fencers know that it is often possible, by taking a step or several steps backwards, to lure an unwary adversary into following incautiously and receiving an unpleasant surprise when he blunders into the danger area. Remember, however, that retreating is relative. If the opponent is outside the measure when he first steps forward, do not attack, as he will certainly parry. If he steps forward from the normal measure, it is then that he is at his most vulnerable: this is the ideal time to attack.

It is not necessary automatically to retire because the opponent steps forward, though many fencers still do so, probably because the habit has become well ingrained during the elementary stages of their footwork training. To attack on the preparation, to stand one's ground and parry, even to step forward with the parry, are all options which frequently throw the opposite party into a state of great confusion.

The Engagement and Change of Engagement

The longer fencing measure now in fashion means that there are fewer attacks on the blade and fewer changes of engagement than formerly; but this is not to say that they can be ignored. For a *coupé dessous*, engage *foible* to *foible* in *quarte*, but do not move the hand and arm away from *sixte*, in which line they should remain throughout. Contact should be made with a diagonally slanted blade and an aggressive authority which will almost certainly elicit a reaction facilitating the cut-over ending in the low line of *octave* inside the blade, the best possible defence to which is the counter of *tierce*. To execute this stroke against the left-hander it is necessary to engage in one's own *sixte*, and the hand and arm should again stay in *sixte* throughout.

The change of engagement can be made from *sixte* to *quarte* and *vice versa*. The double change of engagement, e.g., *sixte* to *quarte* and back again, is an unlikely combination nowadays as the opponent will not leave his blade about for a sufficient length of time.

Double preparations (one preparation followed by another of the same or a different sort) and compound preparations (two preparations performed simultaneously) are not necessarily without value. The gaining of distance and the possibility of provoking an advantageous reaction are the considerations which must be borne in mind.

Beats

All beats can be used as preparations, preferably for simple attacks. They should be made with the fingers, though in *sixte* this technique may be supplemented by a certain amount of wrist action, while in *octave* the wrist only can be used. The beat is usually attended with greater success in the high line, and should be executed with the top third of the blade, i.e., the *foible*, the modern electric blade being heavy enough to guarantee its effectiveness.

Beats can be made before, during or after a step forward; the choice depends entirely on how much time it is thought necessary to gain. To make a beat attack on the opponent's step forward has always been highly effective and is a classic move which should certainly be retained in the repertoire of the modern fencer.

The great value of the return beat is to regain the right of way. It is perhaps better to extend the arm instantly and hope that the opponent runs onto the point rather than to lunge, for if the other fencer perseveres with his own attack, a serious collision may result, or worse still in these inflationary times, broken blades.

The change-beat attack into *quarte* stands some chance of success following a *foible* to *foible* engagement. It should not be attempted into *sixte*, the permanently closed line in modern fencing.

In former times, all manner of compound attacks following beats were witnessed, but today the only serious possibility is the beat, feint-straight-thrust, disengage.

The double beat always had its devotees and is worth a mention. It was accompanied by at least one step, generally two, a comparatively light beat on the first and a stronger one to deflect the blade on the second. All of this was greatly favoured by Charles de Beaumont, the Grand Old Man of British fencing. On any examination course when he was in attendance, the word would go round: 'If he asks you anything about beats, say, "Vary the strength".' It delighted him and was generally worth a few extra marks.

The Froissement before an attack is useless today – the opposing blade is never there long enough for its execution. It has been suggested that it might conceivably be used as a counter-attack with a lunge on an opponent stepping forward with an extended arm. If so, it is best done with a *sixte* engagement and a supinated hand. On the whole, we think it undesirable, as it is likely to lead to spoiling tactics.

The Pressure   With the predominant absence of blade, it would seem to have little relevance to present conditions.

The Coulé   Whether with mere contact, opposition, or as a feint, is outmoded for similar reasons.

Prises-de-fer

A *prise-de-fer* takes the opposing blade from one line to another, or in the case of the *enveloppement*, returns it to the original line. Any *prise-de-fer* is best executed against a straight arm and point that is threatening the target, particularly against an opponent attempting to force his way through a parry or to renew the attack. They may be used offensively (before an attack) or defensively (before a riposte). Owing to the increased modern measure they are likely to be less successful before an attack, though here much will depend on the extent of the opponent's anticipation.

A distinction is generally drawn between compound *prises-de-fer* (two or more in succession, blade contact being maintained throughout) and double *prises-de-fer* (contact lost and regained). At foil there is rarely time or opportunity for more than one. *Prises-de-fer* may be taken in all lines, though in practice some are not realistic, or at best are attended with high risk. To some extent the height of the opponent's weapon is a governing factor. Use the bind or *croisé* against the high hand and blade, the *enveloppement* when lower.

The *Enveloppement* can be performed in the low line, though traditionally it is safest and most effective in *sixte*. It is easiest to dominate the opposing blade in this line, and with this objective in view the circle should be small and 'tight' to minimise the possibility of losing contact.

The Bind If accompanied by a step forward, blade contact should be established with the movement of the front foot, and the diagonal action completed with the grounding of the rear foot. A *balestra* and a bind should be simultaneous. However, in either case there is the danger of inviting a counter-attack, and the bind is better reserved for use preceding a riposte.

Whether it should then be accompanied with a step depends on how quickly the opponent breaks away.

Maximum control is offered from *quarte* to *octave*. This is less true of *septime–sixte* and *sixte–septime* – indeed with two fencers of the same hand, the latter can be extremely dangerous as the opposing point may all too easily slip over the top of the binding weapon, but it is justifiable for a right-hander against a left-hander, as the latter's blade is more readily forced down as the inside line is approached. *Prime–tierce* and vice versa plus *seconde–quarte* may be described as usable in principle, but of small service in a bout.

The Croisé The croisé of *quarte* should never precede an attack, but is very useful at close quarters as a defence against the *remise*. It should be confined to the high-low blade action (never the reverse) with pronated hand and (if there is time to think about it) a slight bending of the legs. *Sixte–croisé* and riposte may have an occasional use against the opponent who persists with his attack and hangs on to the blade, also against the left-hander, or a right-hander with the opposite reactions of opposition. Upwards from *octave* to *sixte* is not practicable, though to lift a left-hander's blade may present some chance of clearing the way for a riposte to his back.

The Croisé of octave The blade is passed over that of the attacker, deflecting it simultaneously with the covered extension of the arm and riposte

PLATE 3   FOIL:

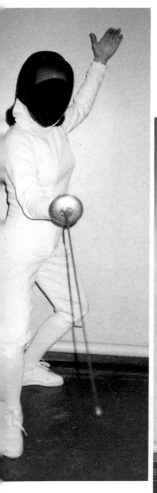

septime

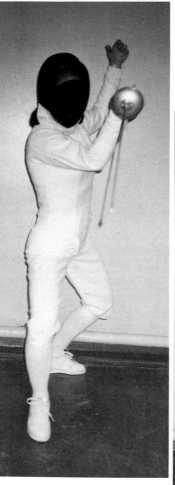

lifted *septime*

octave

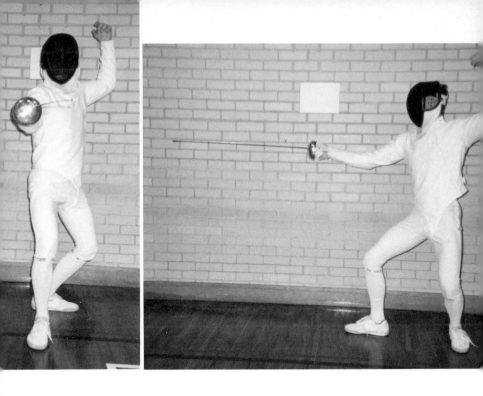

PLATE 4   *EPEE*: (above left and right) *en garde*

(above left) short lunge; (right) lunge – the opponent's view

PLATE 5 *EPEE*: (above) the *flèche*; (below, left) high *prime*; (right) *seconde* or *octave*

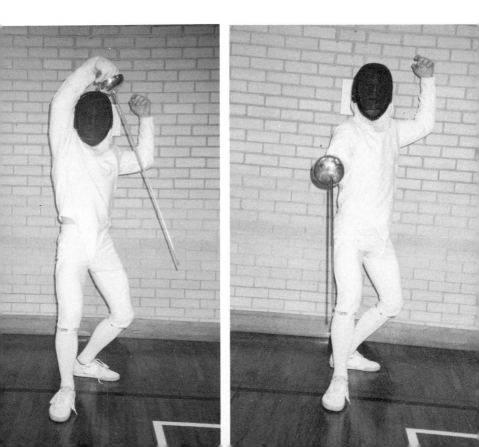

PLATE 6   SABRE: (above, left)
high *prime*; (above, right) *seconde*;
(right) *tierce* (arm slightly extended
as *flèche* is now banned)

into the low line with supinated hand. A winner – particularly as in the low line any failure to deflect the blade completely will probably, at worst, result in a hit off target.

The *Croisé* of *septime* Highly recommended by many authorities as a defence against the left-handed *flècheur*, or indeed any *flèche* attack into the *sixte* line. The blade passes over that of the opponent simultaneously with the arm extension, just as with the *croisé* of *octave*. The hand is not pronated and it is generally wise to take a step back.

The defence against the *prise-de-fer*
The opponent's *prise-de-fer* can be met by either ceding or opposition parries. Archaic examples of the former, largely of interest to the antiquary alone, are ceding to *prime* when the blade has been trapped in *sixte*; ceding to *seconde* when the opponent has forced one's blade into (the old) *quinte*; and ceding to *quarte* as the answer to *quarte-croisé*. As for the *croisé* of *octave*, that is best blocked by an opposition parry of *seconde*.

6: Renewals of Attack

Any stroke can be used as a renewed attack, but as we shall see, not all are generally applicable. Neither is it, as a rule, possible to renew either the riposte or the counter-riposte before the opponent breaks away; and for similar reasons it is hardly practicable to consider the renewal of a counter-attack. As for a second renewal, e.g., the *remise* of the *redoublement* or the *redoublement* of the *redoublement*, all these are pleasant fantasies which can be excluded from the repertoire of the late twentieth century.

All three forms of the renewed attack can be instinctive, but should ideally be premeditated.

The *Remise* Be very wary about a *remise* on the lunge. It occupies a period of fencing time. Indeed, the only really safe *remise* is in the absence of any riposte at all. Against the riposter, today's competitive fencer would do well to forget all about it. A period of fencing time will never be gained in today's ultra-fast exchanges. The only exception to this rule is after being parried in *quarte* when it may be possible to *remise* with *sixte* opposition against a riposte by disengagement. Even so, it is well to remember that the *remise* in the line of *quarte* is generally considered to be the only sober option, both in point of time and because the opposition in *sixte* requires what Bertrand termed a 'contortion.'

For a premeditated *remise* – and this applies to the *redoublement* as well – it is permissible to shorten the initial lunge so that the point can be replaced with a slight forward inclination of the trunk. Care must be exercised, however, to avoid any misjudgment caused by the shortening of the distance.

The slight tap of the leading foot timed to coincide with the *remise* and supposed for some reason to distract the opponent is now outmoded.

The *Redoublement* may be effected *en flèche* or on the lunge, normally by disengagement as the cut-over takes too long, particularly in the latter case. A disengagement from a parry of *sixte* obviously gives the maximum opportunity for a fast, decisive and accurate renewal.

The *Reprise* A possibly unnecessary warning; abstain from making the initial attack in the low line – the whole upper target becomes fearfully vulnerable during the recovery forward.

Nowadays the *reprise* is mostly executed *en flèche*, as an alternative to the second lunge, and as a means of getting within the opponent's distance. Hence the old trick of 'gaining on the *reprise*' (i.e., bringing forward the rear foot until it was practically touching the rear heel), **the purpose being to maintain the distance relative to the opponent**, or if need be to steal distance, is less useful today; the *flèche* is quicker. Similarly, a second *reprise* is no longer used, speed over a relatively short distance being the dominating factor. This in turn necessitates that the blade action of a *reprise* should invariably be simple, unless the distance has been opened.

Fencers used to be seen executing a beat or *prise-de-fer* on their recovery forward, the idea being to protect themselves against a delayed riposte or a stop hit. However, as a successful *reprise* depends very largely on the speed of the recovery forward, we consider that there is little or no time for any such intermediate blade actions. A beat-attack during the final *flèche* is fine in theory as preserving the attacker's priority, but as most fencers know, anything that happens during a *flèche* is likely to be instinctive. However, should a defender step back holding a parry of *sixte*, a recovery forward with strong opposition in *sixte* is helpful preceding a disengagement *en flèche*.

The backward *reprise* is very rarely seen these days and when it does happen is generally instinctive rather than premeditated. Following the parry of an attack in *sixte*, a recovery to guard backwards with a disengagement must be regarded as tactically sound.

7: The *Dérobement*

The *dérobement* is the evasion of the opponent's attempt to attack or take the blade. The *trompement* – and it is amazing how many people still fail to recognise the distinction – is the evasion of the opponent's attempt to parry. The opportunity for the *dérobement* arises when an opponent who is out of distance seeks to protect himself on the advance with some sort of blade preparation. It is well-nigh impossible to avoid a sharp beat unless one can foresee its direction. Even then, it is none too easy. It may be possible, by appearing to offer the blade, to lure one's opponent into stepping forward and attempting to engage, then executing the *dérobement* with a step back if necessary. It follows therefore, that the successful *dérobement* must nearly always be premeditated.

The matter by no means ends there. It is possible that the *dérobement* will have to be compound, as some 'blade attackers' make a double preparation – a beat, followed by a *prise-de-fer*. So the *dérobement*, in its turn, must be by either a one-two, *doublé*, or counter-disengage, or any permutation of these, in either the high or low line.

This must, alas, remain largely in the realm of classical theory. Most modern fencers lack both the skill (handicapped by the orthopaedic grip) and the time essential to perfect the difficult technique to the stage of being able to use it in a bout.

Finally, the *dérobement* must be executed with the point threatening the opponent's target, and with a straight arm which must not at any stage be withdrawn. The opponent, tricked into missing contact with his preparation but continuing his attack, runs straight on to the point. For the triumphant *virtuoso*, one of the pleasantest sensations in fencing.

8: Second Intention and Counter-time

The purists interpret **Second Intention** as Counter-time and nothing but Counter-time. We prefer to give it the wider interpretation, namely, any fencing action intended to draw a reaction from the opponent which enables a further fencing action to be made and, if successful, to score a hit. Counter-time is but one specialised example of this.

Today's fencing is aggressive, athletic and based largely on first intention. There is little place for delightful schemes designed to gain an orthodox reaction from an orthodox opponent. Nevertheless, Second Intention is to some extent possible through the study or knowledge of the opponent. Thus it is possible to draw a riposte from *quarte* and counter-riposte on the lunge by disengagement.

Counter-time itself is the art of drawing the opponent's stop-hit, parrying and riposting. We said in the section on *prises-de-fer* that the bind, when stepping forward, was risky as inviting a stop-hit. Should this form of preparation, therefore, be deliberately employed, as a means of inciting the opponent to stop-hit? Nothing of this sort is impossible, but we cannot honestly recommend the idea as promising success. Counter-time nowadays is very seldom consciously premeditated, because stop-hits have become something of a rarity, on few occasions awarded against the attack.

No stop-hit, no counter-time; so one of the most beautiful and fascinating aspects of fencing with the foil has disappeared into limbo.

9: Broken Time

Broken time may be defined as a loss of fencing time, fundamentally and initially by the attacker, not the defender. The object is to confuse the opponent, so that he either fails to parry at all, or does so in the wrong line. The attack may terminate in the same line as the initial action or in an alternative line. There may be various combinations of the footwork and bladework, but in all cases they must be carefully co-ordinated.

The double cut-over on the advance is one of the most effective examples of broken time in use at foil today, and can be executed with sundry variations:

1 Double cut-over on the advance, lunge with a retracted arm, then place the point.

2 Advance with first half of first cut-over, lunge with retracted arm, and complete cut-over. Second cut-over is executed on the lunge, if needed.

3 Two cut-overs, with a lunge, but delay the last part of the second cut-over for a period of fencing time. The hit arrives after the front foot has been grounded.

The above examples all have the effect of making the defender lose time in his turn.

In the following example, the switch of direction has the same effect.

With a step or *balestra*, take the opponent's blade into 'old-fashioned' *quinte*. (The hand remains in the *sixte* line but is pronated and the blade is laid diagonally on the opponent's, taking his blade into the low line.) Then with the lunge, feint a cut-over into the low line, then cut-over into the high line.

10: Tactics

A good deal of this has been said before, but it will bear repetition, both to refresh the memory and as a convenient reference. There are certain points, too, which may be queried or qualified.

To begin with, there has been a great deal of traditional and highly well-intentioned advice about reconnaissance preparations, false attacks and the like, designed to ascertain the opponent's probable reactions, favourite parries and general style. The Italians even had a name for it, *scandaglio*, or the 'sounding-out'. And after that one was supposed to make a stately progress through the various stages of simple attacks, compound attacks, preparations when the former proved unsuccessful, and so on, up to the more refined arts of second intention.

A bout lasts six minutes at most; and what these airy counsellors seemed to forget was that during that entire time the opponent, so far from maintaining a convenient docility, was probably charging at one with obviously felonious intent. It is clear, therefore, that the *scandaglio* must at best be a supplement to a psychological assessment beforehand. You may have faced a particular fencer before; if not, take every opportunity of observing each one of his other bouts, despite what some coaches say about allowing the mind to go completely blank when off the *piste*, or indulging in some species of yoga-like meditation.

Never over-elaborate. Never abandon the straight-forward action if it is proving successful. Keep repeating it until the opponent finds the answer. In the somewhat unlikely event of having scored four hits in quick succession by simple disengagements, it can prove fatal to try something else merely for the sake of it. You can be too clever.

We have said more that once already, and will stress it again, that the most favourable time for any attack is on the opponent's step forward (see *Attacks* pp. 20 and 23). To attack or to *flèche* on the opponent's recovery to guard, when his vigilance is supposed to have relaxed, depends entirely on the circumstances, in particular, of course the distance.

We also said earlier that the step should be short, but that does not mean that it must become mechanically uniform. To confuse the adversary's sense of distance, it can be lengthened or reduced still further, in the one case stealing within his distance, in the other luring him forward within one's own measure. The vulnerability of an opponent weak in *octave* can be increased by shifting one's position across the *piste* and attacking from the angle he will find even more awkward.

Another way of confusing the opponent's sense of distance, is by fencing with the arm more extended or more retracted than is generally the case. The latter encourages him to come too close; the former may have the same effect when the arm is restored to its original position.

The opponent may also be deceived by a deliberate disguise of one's own style. He may be baffled and his alertness blunted by numerous blade and foot actions at a pace significantly slower than normal. His reactions may not be equal to a sudden, unexpected burst of speed. The execution of both parries and attacks different from those usually favoured may encourage him to adopt both offensive and defensive actions ill-suited to the situation when 'normal service is resumed' with recourse to one's standard armoury.

Of course, only the fencer himself can decide what is relevant to the actual conditions prevailing; and a note of caution must be sounded. We are speaking here of controlling, indeed modifying, well-rehearsed and trained reflexes of speed, distance and reaction which in the heat of combat, with a dozen distracting influences, is no easy matter and may spell danger.

The choice between simple, circular and half-circular parries depends in the majority of cases on the position of the opponent's blade. The greater its lateral distance, the less feasible is the circular or even the half-circular parry. *Prime* is always an option against the high attack inside.

Repeated simple parries can draw the one-two, finishing for preference in the *quarte* line to allow the direct riposte. Alternatively, to an attack ending in *sixte* the reply could be by *sixte*.

Counter parries will encourage the *doublé*, which, according to tradition, was met in the final line by a covered stop-hit in *sixte*. It is better now to make the initial circular parry in *sixte*, then take the final action by a *croisé* of *octave*.

To some extent fencers may be assigned to certain categories.

The solid defensive type who obstinately refuses to respond to feints, false invitations, false attacks, is a problem. The only course is to work on him, giving him no peace and hoping that in the end his patience will wear thin. But it is difficult, and time and proficient execution are the only answers.

Get within the measure of **the unusually tall opponent**. His long reach is his strong suit, so don't allow him to use it. Energetic footwork and if possible, attacks on the blade must be employed to allow further action at relatively close quarters. In other words, you must risk being hit to score a hit. Conversely, **the small, bustling, light-footed fencer** must be kept at a respectful distance by counter-attacks, and attacks on his preparation.

A beat in *quarte* followed by a cut-over downwards and backward, the attack finishing in octave, is useful against **those who either keep their hand too high** or cannot parry *octave* or *seconde*.

The habitual 'remiser'   The *remise* (the replacing of the point in the same line as the parry) is now largely accidental, although by some presidents miscalled 'the continuation of the attack', when they should really have analysed the phrase as 'an attack *mal paré*'. Whatever the competence of the president, the answers are to take wider parries, a *prise-de-fer* following the parry, or even two parries against the heavy-handed fencer who really tries to force his way through the defence.

The habitual redoubler   *Redoublements* are academically easier to the inside line following any parry in an outside line.

Today's fencer, however, will redouble from any parry to any line which is open. It matters not what parry is taken – he will redouble anyway, generally with mobility involving an additional foot action forward or backward, often culminating in a *flèche*.

The defender may confidently employ any *prise-de-fer* as an alternative to two parries. Better still is the instant riposte and best of all, the breaking or closing of distance will be found to be as effective a response as any. In the last two cases the second parry should always be attempted.

There are always some fencers who invariably prepare their attacks by a step forward – today, of course, with the lengthened measure, this is virtually a standard practice. Our advice is not to be intimidated; on the contrary, stand your ground, or even take a step forward. This will take control as it is instinctive to step back when your opponent steps forward and it will be an unwelcome alteration of distance which will rob him of space and acceleration.

Similar advice applies to those confronted by **the automatic *flècheur***. Do not listen to those who talk about parrying/riposting/stop-hitting 'on the retreat', i.e., while running backwards. As above, be obstinate: don't run away, but parry *prime* with no more than one step backwards. (See also *Against the Left hander*, below). Against the right-hander, the defence should be varied according to the circumstances; *quinte* is another alternative.

The maddening character generally described as **the 'rusher'** demands necessary, if unmerited, attention. Inordinately fast and fit (or at least he should be), he can only score by simple attacks usually preceded by a clawing action at the blade, charitably described as a preparation.

Your parry may have to be very strong, which renders the detached parry and riposte difficult. One answer may be the *prise-de-fer* if he holds on to your blade; the disengagement may be dangerous – he will be all ready for the *remise*, either well-ingrained or instinctive.

In any case, you will have to maintain the measure and play him for distance. Like most fencers, he is generally disconcerted by a parry with a step forward.

If time is running out and one is not ahead on hits, adopt desperate measures, attack into the attack and hope.

An attempt may also be made to stop-hit by *dérobement*, but this is extremely difficult. The whole business is dreary, often involving an apparently endless chase up and down the *piste*, but after all, not every fencer can be expected to be good enough to be a public entertainer.

11: Against the Left-hander

Sooner or later the left-hander throws his dread shadow across the pages of every fencing book. At one time, masters tried to steady the nerves of their anxious pupils by assuring them (with sublime indifference to the truth) that it was 'all just the same'. It is not the same – apart from anything else, the relative angle of the targets is different, and a number of things are worth bearing in mind when facing an opponent of the opposite hand. One must always keep in mind that fencing is – and we quote – 'always straight lines and circles'.

It may be a truism to repeat that the left-hander is vulnerable in his low line and *octave* area, but he certainly is and also on the top of his left shoulder and back, particularly if he leans forward with a semi-crouching position. A step to one side may further expose these danger-areas to an unwelcome attack from an awkward angle.

Against a fencer of the same hand, any attack which is not simple requires an even number of blade actions, i.e., two or four to outstrip his defence. Against an opponent with the opposite hand, the number is uneven. One action or three will find one of his open lines, e.g., low-high-low; but the permutations are endless.

Some fencers find defence against the left-hander more troublesome than attack. We suggest that *tierce* as opposed to *seconde* is more reliable, the riposte going direct into the open line. The angle of the blade to the target is what matters, i.e., 'straight lines and circles' and the point should be kept as near to the target as possible at all times, particularly in defence.

From *quarte* the riposte should go:

a   To the small of the back, angulated.

b   Under the arm.

c   To his *sixte* line.

d   To the top of his shoulder towards his back, with a well lifted hand, which may be pronated or supinated according to both choice and circumstance.

From *sixte* the options are the same, apart, of course from the direct riposte, which is made into *quarte*.

In both cases the riposte by disengagement is also a possibility.

Lifted *septime* is an option, but gives little time for the riposte. *Octave* can be used but as this takes the blade across one's target, one has little time, if any, to complete a riposte. We suggest that the safest parry against the left-hander is *prime*, with the possible riposte to the front of the target.

This means that you will either have to take a step back or withdraw front foot to rear foot and stand up as you parry.

Counter-Action, contraction, and **circular** parries are of general use to all, but are rather more effective against the left-hander. The counter-action parry is simply a circular parry taken the wrong way round, e.g., anti-clockwise in *sixte* and vice versa in *quarte*.

The contraction parry is similar, but is done with the arm fully extended. Then the elbow is bent and the sword-arm is withdrawn by means of a ceding parry to bring the opponent's blade into the opposite line to that in which it started. This cuts the line and generally exposes the left-hander's back to a riposte. It should be emphasised that the defender's point remains high throughout – the contraction parry is not a *prise-de-fer*.

The circular parry is exactly what it says – it collects the opponent's blade with a circular action, either clockwise or anti-clockwise, travelling under the opposing blade in the high line, over in the low line.

Part Three

EPEE

1: Attacks

'*Make all attacks with an advance, all defence with a retreat.*' So went the word, long years ago. Obviously, there must be exceptions, but given the comprehensive target, it is still not a bad general principle. May we also humbly suggest, in face of what at times appears to be a thriving school of heresy, that it is upon the whole, better to keep the sword-arm well extended and properly covered?

While attacks (and for that matter, ripostes) can be directed to any part of the target, it is advisable to vary one's options within the limits of the situation, bearing in mind that after a parry the original attacker's target is more widely exposed.

There are in fact more attacks to the body and fewer to the arm nowadays, because contemporary fencers close in for the actual hit through lack of confidence (probably justified) in their own technique. If they stayed at the classic *épée* distance, they might score fewer hits but would receive far less.

The surprise element at *épée* is vital, because of the predominance of counter-attacks. So, on the rare occasions when it is possible, attack from immobility. In any, case, avoid 'telegraphing' your intentions.

As Vass endlessly repeats, all offensive actions can be executed from riposting distance, lunging distance, or long distance (outside lunging distance). In cases where a choice is possible, is the lunge or the *flèche* to be preferred? Ideally, the matter should depend wholly on distance and the tactics of the opponent, and the *flèche* be employed as a surprise factor only, but at present it is very much in the ascendant.

It is of the utmost importance to keep the head still. At the outset, most fencers tend to throw it back. On the other hand, it should not be allowed to drop forward. The *flècheur*, as we have said earlier, should fix his eyes on a point about a hand's height above his opponent's head. This helps to keep the head still.

The *flèche* on the opponent's recovery to guard, once highly recommended, is now of little service, as fewer fencers are seen to use the lunge these days.

A short lunge at the arm with an angulated blade is fine if opponents and the fashion of the times allow. The alternative to the *flèche*, the step and lunge, would be one of the best ways to reach an opponent's arm, were not so many fencers in the habit of simply running away.

One cannot therefore entirely blame the modern obsession with the *flèche*. If reduced to making a *flèche* at the arm, go for the inner arm, as an inaccurate attack could still hit the trunk even by accident. Whatever the target area aimed at, the *flècheur* should control the adversary's blade with opposition – if he can.

Only after prolonged practice are even the very best fencers capable of *flèche* attacks with opposition to the lower part of the hand.

To disguise an angulated attack, the direction of the blade should in principle be unaltered until the last possible moment.

However, some fencers are able to co-ordinate their hand and eye much better than others. Much will depend upon the individual and the approach of his or her coach. At worst, there should be no angulation until the rear foot is firmly on the floor at the conclusion of any step forward.

Following an angulated attack with a lunge, be sure to withdraw quickly, as the action will have exposed part of the sword arm. This is a particular hazard in attacking any part of the body while at close quarters, when, in extreme cases, the arm will form an arrow-head (∧) with the elbow on top and a 'flick' hit, or anything likely to score is in order.

Attacks into the low line inevitably expose a good deal of the upper target, so, with the present tendency to shorten the *épée* measure, they are none too common. However, if attempted at all, they should be used sparingly and *en flèche*, although most *flèche* attacks go into the high line.

A straight thrust to the body is dangerous, calling for a double hit unless time has been clearly gained. An attack to the knee or thigh is better and a direct attack to the foot may occasionally take the opponent by surprise.

The disengagement, whether as a simple attack or in the course of a compound action, is theoretically as small and v-shaped as at foil, but the additional weight of the *épée* renders it a good deal more circular. Theoretically, of course, it is best on the opponent's engagement or attempt to engage. But in the first place, no-one will engage in the full *quarte* position, and if they make a diagonal contact, a disengagement is impossible.

In theory again, the counter-disengagement is 'all right' on the opponent's attempt to change the line. But few fencers nowadays attempt to engage the blade until the final hit. This is worth remembering as a form of very late opposition and covering against a double hit.

The cut-over: the time factor of one twenty-fifth of a second separating hits militates against its use at *épée*. At foil, the conventions allow significantly longer for its execution. However, it is a mistake to dismiss the cut-over as wholly inapplicable. It may be effective, particularly when the withdrawal needed to clear the point is restricted to a minimum.

Compound Attacks

It is a good principle to keep the épée attacks as simple as possible. Speed, aggression and timing will take the modern fencer a long way today.

Nevertheless, everything will depend on the circumstances. All fencing actions have always been possible in all eras; only, with the passage of time and differing styles and tactics, certain strokes become either more or less applicable. In the end, only the individual fencer on the *piste* can decide for him or herself what is or what is not, relevant to the actions of the fencer opposite.

We stress that, as with simple attacks, the sword-arm should be kept extended throughout. Voices have been raised, claiming that feints should be made with a bent arm, the extension coinciding with the final of the attack. Such a method loses both time and accuracy.

No feints should be made to the outside arm – it is impossible to hit without being hit as one exposes one's own sword-arm.

Feinting to the inner arm is a different matter, as this will usually draw some kind of reaction. For the record – feints directed to opposite extremes of the target will very probably draw a reaction.

A rapid lowering and lifting of the blade to 'indicate' **feints while advancing is highly likely to provoke some kind of response, physical or mental**.

Do not be too quick to laugh the compound attack out of court. Often the one-two-three will work if you meet someone foolish enough to keep following the blade. The trouble is that this sort of fencer will probably retreat anyway, and not too many hits are scored against a fencer who is running away.

2: Defence

The positions of *sixte* and *octave* are to be regarded as starting points for any defence at *épée*. Ninety per cent of *épée* parries are with opposition and to parry with the lower half of the blade is about right with this weapon. Parries are 'flatter' than at foil, the point normally being at shoulder-level in the high line, but it can be raised to the height of one's own head against wide, ill-controlled blade actions. Parries should be taken with the arm partially extended and the elbow covered. From time to time one still hears references to the 'straight-arm' guard and the attempt to parry with a fully straightened arm. The old-timers did it, but they had both time and skill on their side. Cadence then, and we are talking oʃ over twenty years ago, was a great deal slower. Today, a fencer whose arm is too far forward and misses his parry is almost certain to be hit.

Epéeists today are often uncertain as to whether they should always step back when parrying. A retreat indeed gives added security if pure defence is the sole consideration, but any offensive action is correspondingly more difficult.

As at foil, possibly the most efficient parry to the *flèche* is *prime*. The level of the point depends on the height of the hand. Knee height is about right for the orthodox position, but it can be any height as long as it deflects the opponent's blade.

Many former experts advocated the stronger *seconde* and the counter of *seconde* to the corresponding *octave* parries, but most modern fencers prefer *octave*, due to the fact that pronation of the hand with an orthopaedic grip is not only difficult but for some impossible. When using these low line parries or guards the point of one's sword should be directed at the height of the opponent's leading thigh. Anything lower, will only lead to a time delay with the next offensive action. Similarly, *tierce* is stronger than *sixte*, but suffers from the same objection as *seconde*, the difficulty of pronation.

Quarte fails to give safety either for attack or defence as it always leaves the outside of the attacking arm and the outside low line area vulnerable. Some say that *quarte* should be used against an attack to the body, keeping the elbow close to the hip and lowering the forearm, but it must be regarded as a self-defence reaction parry, not to be cultivated. Lifted *septime* or a counter of *sixte* are much safer.

The 'beat parry' of *quarte*, often recommended against an attack to the wrist or hand is not, properly speaking, a parry at all. In the vast majority of cases it is not practicable and less than safe. If attempted at all, it should be with the use of the wrist, not the forearm.

Sixte is efficient all round, easy for launching attacks and its related parries and there is no reason at all to alter the view that *sixte* and counter of *sixte* are fundamental to a sound defence. The counter of *sixte* with a lifted point has the virtue of 'collecting' the opponent's blade and slipping it down towards the guard.

Once again there is much dispute on the size of the circle, to what extent the wrist should supplement the finger action, whether the forearm should be used as well, and whether these considerations should be further influenced by the part of the target that is being defended. We take a severely practical view – the blade action should be sufficiently large to collect the opponent's blade, but kept as small as possible. Technically, if the attack is to the inside wrist, the fingers alone should be used, but this is impossible with the orthopaedic grip.

Septime, or rather, lifted *septime* should not be used as a preparation of attack. It should be regarded as purely defensive and combined with a step back, not a step forward. Lifted *septime* defends the inside low line, and to a certain extent, the inside upper target. The point should be level with the opponent's thigh.

Counter of *octave* has been suggested as preferable to high line defence on the grounds that the latter exposes the underarm. True; but why ignore the fact that either way, it is a fifty-fifty business?

Parries with the *coquille*: use them if you can learn to do so. They are particularly valid against attacks to the wrist and forearm, where they are even more effective than the blade. Now, when using the *coquille*, the parry of *quarte* is legitimate.

Defence with the guard is most effective when the attacker, with an extended arm, keeps pecking away at wrist or hand, especially when his attack is directed underneath. Just drop the guard, allow the *coquille* to deflect the opponent's blade, and keeping your point on the target, extend the arm and hit.

Semi-circular parries, or 'destructing' parries as the Hungarians call them, are fine, but should be confined to the outside line, *sixte* to *octave* and vice versa. The wrist not the forearm, should be used in the semi-circular parry of *octave*. It is legitimate to lower the hand when defending the foot.

If one should be marooned in *quarte*, semi-circular *septime* against either a high or low attack is better than counter of *quarte* or trying to take *octave*.

Diagonal parries (e.g. *sixte–septime*) are risky, but like a number of other things in life, all right if you can get away with them. They may be used by a sufficiently competent fencer, but they are highly vulnerable when strong opposition is applied. Because of the blade angle, the parry may then have to be taken with the *foible*.

Defence against the flèche   The best option is counter of *sixte* with a step back, holding the blade until the point has passed, then riposte to flank or leg; the riposte at arm is too difficult. But with a pistol grip, the circular parry is too slow and *prime*, standing up, must be the answer.

Successive parries   The best advice here is to vary them in opposite directions as much as possible and not let the opponent familiarise himself with a set pattern.

3: Ripostes

Ripostes should be made with opposition. To the arm, they should for preference be made with opposition and angulation; it is only when riposting under the hand or arm that the two can be combined. If the blade is 'flat' when parrying, a riposte to the arm with opposition is possible if you have the correct technique. Ripostes to the arm are the most generally favoured of the direct ripostes. If intending to riposte to the shoulder, it will help to lift the point shoulder high in the parry.

Ripostes may certainly be delivered *en flèche*, even over a short distance. 'Anything for a hit' is good fencing, as long as we can get away with it.

Ripostes by counter-disengagement and disengagement are seldom viable and should certainly not be made from *octave* to the high line. It leaves one uncovered. The cut-over, however, may occasionally be used as a surprise tactic, often with great success, but beware of the danger of a renewal; it is always accompanied with considerable risk.

Compound Ripostes

All compound ripostes at foil can be adapted to *épée*, and fencers ought to be prepared to use them should the occasion arise; they are difficult at this weapon and the chances of success are exceedingly remote but they should always be kept in mind.

Counter Ripostes

It is fairly safe more or less to ignore counter ripostes. If the opportunity does occur, they should be directed at the sword-arm and the parries taken well forward. Counter ripostes *en flèche* can only really happen if the opponent is retiring at full speed.

Counter Ripostes in Counter-time

Years ago, Crosnier worked out a phrase so complicated as to make one's mind reel. It went something like this:

1   The attacker, when parried, recovers to guard with a circular or half-circular parry to protect himself against the riposte.

2   The defender, realising this, next time deceives the parry with an indirect riposte.

3 The attacker, recognising the ploy in his turn, only starts to parry and having drawn the riposte, stop hits (or makes a delayed *redoublement* – phrase it whatever way that you like).

4 Finally the defender, even smarter, only feints an indirect riposte to draw the stop hit, parries it and 'counter ripostes'.

(Though it isn't a true counter riposte, the attacker not having parried the riposte. To be pedantic, it should be classed as the riposte following the parry of a renewed attack.)

We can only say that any fencer who can perform all this under match conditions, or any president who can recognise and correctly phrase it, will be deservedly rewarded by a signed complimentary copy of this book.

4: Counter-attacks

Counter-attack as often as possible, but it is essential to remain covered. By all means stop hit on a simple attack if it can be done successfully. Very often today's counter attack takes the form of an attack into the attack.

Otherwise it should be accompanied by a retreat. Ignore ponderous instructions about how one should withdraw the rear foot simultaneously with the stop hit, then retract the front foot, etc. Use any form of footwork that you are able to do and is advantageous to you.

Stop hits to the trunk are all very well, but will always increase the danger of a double hit. Hand, arm, shoulder, mask are more vulnerable to the counter-attack. The foot is a tempting target, particularly when the opponent is advancing – it must be almost the nearest part of his body to you. Whether to stop-hit above or below the arm depends on the height of the opponent's hand. While attacking to the wrist and forearm, angulation may be necessary. When an attack is aimed at the body, a stop-hit aimed at the opponent's wrist may be possible. To stop hit by disengagement on the opponent's attempt to take the blade, is difficult.

The same will apply to the time hit (a stop hit with opposition on the final action of the attack). For example, the very stylish time hit by the *croisé* of *octave* is splendid if the fencer can execute it with success. So is the time-hit in *sixte* to the mask accompanied by a slight retirement, when one has been attacked to the chest in the *sixte* line; however, the high speed of today's modern attacks constitutes a serious threat, so that the stop hit without blade contact is far safer and permits greater mobility.

Another classical action was the *rassemblement*, much favoured by the

PLATE 7 SABRE: (above left) *quinte* (front view); (above right) *quinte* (side view); (below) the sabre lunge

PLATE 8   *EPEE*: (above) counter-attack to knee;

(above) attack to the mask;   (below) stop hit to the leg

PLATE 9   (above) An attempt to stop-hit at the Martini *Epée* challenge in London.
H.W.F. Hoskyns is the President; (below) *Epée*: a *flèche* attack

PLATE 10   FOIL: (above) a *flèche* attack; (below) the stop–hit known as the 'boar's thrust'

old-time *épée* fencer. To attempt the stop hit to the top of the wrist, he withdrew his leading foot until both heels were touching, and stood upright while placing the point. It would be pleasant to see this put into practice by the technically able today when the conditions allowed.

We will not discuss the renewals of counter-attacks. If the first attempt fails, you are most likely to be hit anyway, but in Section 6 we give a conceivable example.

5: Preparations of Attack

Footwork

Steps forward and back should constantly be varied in length to help to gain the advantage in distance, so long as our basic rule is not violated, which stresses the necessity of maintaining body-balance.

Engagements

Do not lend themselves to anything like the variety and subtlety which was formerly the case – but a strong engagement in *quarte* brings a reflex opposition which gives the chance of a hit elsewhere. The engagement itself must be made by wrist flexion only and an unmoved sword-arm, the blade being angulated well across. Similar reactions may also follow strong contact in *octave*, but here again the position of the hand must be watched.

Engagements which 'collect', that is, pass under or over the opponent's blade to make contact on the opposite side, are often more effective still in preparing an attack.

Beats

Beats confer the opening which in turn gives the advantage in time which is vital at *épée*. The opened line needs no further comment; but even then when the blade has been definitely deflected, a beat not seldom induces a rapid defensive reflex.

A most distinguished master of our acquaintance regarded it as almost axiomatic to take or attack the blade before committing oneself to an attack. This is sound enough advice in principle, but fencers should be wary of an excessive use of the beat. The absence of conventions may result in drawing the very stop-hit it is supposed to preclude.

Before the beat can be made at all, it is often necessary to close the measure with feints and false attacks to bring the blade within reach.

The movement of the attacking blade must be powerful but limited, so that it is impossible to avoid and the blade does not move too far away. Any beat inevitably takes the point away from the target, and this deviation must be corrected and the blade returned to the line before the attack.

Any beat further than one-third of the way down the blade means that the hand is so far extended as to invite a stop-hit.

It is well to remember that beats can be delivered from four directions, upwards and downwards as well as laterally. The last example we do not advise. The majority of beat attacks are made to the sword arm and the straight thrust underneath the arm is potentially devastating, but it must be prepared by an upward beat and executed with a straight arm. Otherwise, severe angulation is needed. When little deflection has occurred, those who can hit underneath the arm en flèche constitute a small minority.

At times an opposite reaction will be gained; the downward beat will bring the opponent's blade up, and vice versa. The following attack must be adapted accordingly.

Fencers may execute the beat in whatever line they please. When beating into what we rather misleadingly call quarte, the hand (as when engaging in this way) must definitely remain in sixte and the attack on the blade delivered with a powerful wrist and hand action.

A low-line beat may be followed by an attack to the foot, the inside low target, or the thigh, or underneath the wrist. A lifted beat in septime is highly advantageous, and the beat in seconde (if the grip will allow it) is more forceful than octave. But be warned here, do not extend the sword-arm in the process.

A beat is generally simultaneous with any preliminary foot action, but occasionally try a beat from immobility, if the distance will allow, and exploit any reaction – or lack of it. When stepping forward, the beat may coincide with the placing of either foot. A beat with the balestra or a beat-flèche gains most time. When the flèche is in prospect, it is advisable to make the beat as late as possible.

Opportunities for the change-beat are rare, the blades generally being so far apart. We prefer to call it a 'change of relationship', the beat being delivered on the side opposite to that of the direct beat. The circumstances are most favourable when the opponent has lifted his point rather than keeping the blade strictly in line.

A corresponding beat in the low line may be executed when the opponent's blade is at a steeper angle than usual.

The strength of the beat can always be modified, either to open the line or to provoke a return beat. Hence the double beat can be useful if the opponent will only allow it, and keep his blade somewhere within reach. The first beat should coincide with the step, the second, markedly stronger, should immediately precede the attack which should be unleashed without the slightest inhibition.

For the defence against a beat, strong opposition is necessary, and a stop-hit may be aimed against the arm. Maintain an extended arm and stop-hit by disengagement if the opponent is not too quick for you; otherwise keep the arm straight and either step in, or beat a tactical retreat.

Prises-de-fer

All examples of *prises-de-fer*, including double and compound, are applicable, given the right conditions, and always assuming that the sword-arm does not finish in some hopelessly exposed position. However, opportunities are now somewhat infrequent. A high proportion of swordsmen rely on what is disparagingly termed pig-sticking, jabbing at the arm and then leaping away, and it is only possible thoroughly to master the opposing blade at relatively close quarters.

There has been a recent tendency, however, among those able to close the measure, to indulge in tremendously wide circular or semi-circular blade actions in the course of an attack or riposte being directed almost vertically downwards at close quarters. Again, we have seen a bind to *prime* from a very high *sixte*, the hit going to the body. A parry of *prime* and a bind only half-way to *sixte*, the hit going to the trunk, may well represent a reflex action. All this at least has the advantage of safeguarding oneself and keeping the opponent's point well away.

There are only four real answers to the *prise-de-fer*; the ceding parry, the opposition parry, the retreat with opposition – or incontinent flight.

6: Renewals of Attack

Fencing theory recognises three varieties of renewed attacks, the *remise*, *redoublement* and *reprise*. They have latterly become mainly instinctive, the majority of *épée* fencers and even presidents being unable to distinguish between an attack and its renewal, with the result that all three merge together in a sloppy miscellany.

The renewed attack may follow any necessary step or *balestra*, and the *reprise* may be executed with a lunge or *flèche*.

The question of whether one should *remise* or *redouble* on the lunge or during the recovery is entirely a matter of distance. Vass gives examples of one renewal during the recovery and another on the retreat if the opponent persists in following up and comes within distance.

To renew with compound blade actions of one or two feints, including disengagements and counter-disengagements, is only valid if there is time and the opponent becomes too engrossed in his successive parries.

Time and distance are vital in the execution of renewals as anywhere else. Hence, if time allows, introduce the renewal with a beat which will provoke a reaction, as will a *prise-de-fer*; but it is unusual today for an opponent to keep the sword arm straight, especially while retreating, so a bind, particularly valuable before a *flèche*, may not be feasible. However, if the weapon should be maintained in line, try to renew with opposition.

The *remise* is now accidental rather than premeditated. Too many presidents and fencers are heard referring to the 'continuation of the attack'. There can be no such thing. There can only be one attack, and unless there is a distinct secondary blade action, the attack must have been incompletely parried.

Not many fencers would think of a *remise* to the body following an attack to the arm which had been parried, even if they could do it; far more likely to be successful is a *redoublement* to the body. A *remise* to the arm is always possible, especially if the opponent ripostes.

To redouble by disengagement and opposition on a direct riposte, as has been suggested, seems ambitious, to put it mildly. Against a riposte, defend in any way that you can and consider yourself lucky. A delayed riposte is a different matter – then, of course, *redouble* anywhere.

The *reprise*: an initial lunge, slightly shortened, obviously facilitates the recovery and *flèche*.

A short *flèche* is more aggressive than a second lunge, but it need not necessarily be supposed that the *flèche* alone offers a serious chance of success with the *reprise*. A *flèche* will certainly be mandatory if the opponent is continuously retreating. Then, the blade contact should be maintained as long as possible. The renewal can be by straight thrust if the first attack has merely been avoided and not parried at all.

Having attacked the advanced target with a half or full lunge, the *reprise en flèche* may be directed at the body.

The *remise* and *redoublement* of the riposte are applicable against those counter-riposting with a reprising action. The most opportune moment is just as the *flèche* has commenced. A time-hitting technique with opposition gives increased protection, so cover if there is time.

Renewed Counter Attacks

Among average fencers, these will be reflex actions; with the class fencer, a conscious second intention. Such renewals can be by any of the three R's.

Example: A simple counter-attack is parried, but the opponent either delays his riposte or loses control of the blade. The counter-attack is then renewed in any fashion dictated by distance and the opponent's reaction or absence of reaction.

Defence against renewals

It is advisable not to riposte mechanically while the opponent's blade is still a potential threat; it is better to hold the parry until the blade is past the target.

This may be expedited with a step forward with the parry and a riposte with opposition.

Alternatively, use repeated parries and compound or double *prises-de-fer* if and when there is sufficient time to gain effective control of the blade.

7: The *Dérobement*

The *dérobement* should not entirely be ignored, although attempts to take the blade are much less common than formerly. Moreover, we must avoid thinking of 'takings' as being precisely recognisable and as clear-cut as they used to be, and allow for the fact that the opponent's actions are far more rugged and aggressive. The moderns rely on beats rather than *prises-de-fer*, and it is a truism to say that it is harder to evade a beat than a bind or *enveloppement*.

Nevertheless, as we have repeatedly stressed, all known fencing actions are legitimate at any weapon, given only the right conditions. Be alert for the attempted bind into *octave*.

This is the exception to the rule, for it is frequently used by opponents anxious to clear the blade from their own target. Remember that there is no rule about priority as at foil. Nothing prevents you freeing your blade after contact has been made and immediately threatening your opponent, often in the high line and while on the retreat.

Fewer fencers these days favour a *prise-de-fer* following a parry. Lifted parries are regarded as a superior form of protection, and they are less easy to deceive with a *dérobement*. Ceding parries, or a retreat with strong opposition of blade are in most cases the safer options to a *prise-de-fer*.

The defence against the *dérobement* is the double *prise-de-fer*, often executed on the advance and ending with a lunge to the body if sufficient distance has been gained. As already mentioned above, if the opponent's sword is finally carried down into *octave* with the second blade action, the threatening point is taken out of harm's way. In many cases this will be a panic reaction, not deliberate like the lifted parries, but it may help you out in an emergency.

While dealing with a persistent *dérober*, watch your distance very carefully.

8: Broken Time

One twenty-fifth of a second allows no time to exploit this theory in any specific fashion, so broken time must be regarded as purely accidental at *épée*. There is therefore no need to discuss it either here or later in the tactical section.

9: Second Intention and Counter-Time

Second intention in the wider sense is largely instinctive at *épée*. But pure counter-time, i.e., deliberately drawing a counter-attack, parrying and riposting, may be classed as malice aforethought.

Some masters distrust counter-time at *épée* because of the lack of conventions, but most admit that it has its uses, provided the opponent's tactics are first thoroughly analysed.

Invitations intended to provoke a stop-hit generally involve altering the distance by one or more steps. Another possibility is the *croisé*, or an attempted engagement to draw a stop-hit by disengagement.

A feint in the low line almost invariably draws a stop-hit. The feint should be at the knee or the foot, not merely low in the foil sense, and the blade should be maintained in the low line as long as possible. The parry should be taken well forward, with the *coquille*, rather than the blade, used as much as possible. A parry of *sixte* and a riposte *en flèche* make a fitting climax.

Sometimes a feint, particularly the example described above, will draw a sudden *flèche*. It is essential to keep one's head. If you see a chance, stop-hit; if not, parry and riposte.

The question of whether a *prise-de-fer* should be interposed between parry and riposte is answered by our now familiar slogan : 'Anything in the fencing repertoire is viable – but it will depend on who does what.'

The feint-in-time is a compound stop-hit against the fencer using counter-time and inviting a stop-hit. The idea is that the latter executes a premeditated parry that is deceived; but such subtlety is likely to occur by accident.

The stop-hit in counter time, or in other words, the stop-hit on the opponent's stop-hit: a good example is to draw the stop-hit beneath one's own arm, then stop-hit on top of your opponent's arm while simultaneously parrying with the *coquille*.

10: Tactics

The grip may well have some bearing on fencing tactics, particularly where the *épée* is concerned. For that matter, orthopaedic grips at both foil and *épée* are generally available in three sizes, but may have to be modified still further to suit the individual. A pistol grip is recommended for the épéeist with small fingers or less well developed muscles in hand and wrist. The French grip is now as rare at *épée* as at foil, but it allows the swordsman a choice of alternatives. It may be held further back to increase the reach. Raymond Paul, in the sixties, was a great exponent of this. Some of the old-time virtuosos even held it by the pommel, but this requires a remarkable sense of co-ordination between hand and eye. Charles de Beaumont, a master of the latter technique, did not exclude other unorthodox grips. In one example, the forefinger, flat on the side of the handle, directed the weapon, which was manipulated by the thumb and last fingers. This method gives great accuracy in hits at the wrist, but sacrifices both speed and precision in defence. Such refinements can only be exploited by very experienced fencers, but all should be prepared to experiment and not flinch from attempting new techniques.

What is essential at *épée* is a grip which promotes vigorous blade actions and a hit with authority. 'Treat it as a gun' was the advice given by Giuseppe Mangiarotti, the famous Italian *maestro*.

For the basic blade position when *en garde*, orthodox *sixte* is admirable, while maintaining the blade diagonally across the body.

Fencing actions are either purely instinctive, controlled by reflex action, or premeditated. The natural reflexes must be controlled. Only thus can a fencer control his cadence and he who controls the cadence, controls the bout.

Cadence itself controls time, distance and rhythm, and an advanced fencer should be able to modify any of these three, either collectively, or individually. Cadence should be continually altered, as an additional obstacle to the smooth development of the opponent's strategy. The deliberate inversion of cadence is equally important at foil and sabre. Thus a sudden very fast attack may well score after the opponent has been soothed by a succession of slower steps, feints and false attacks. The opposite is also true. Most of us have seen a master fencer discomfit his opponent, conditioned by a series of lightning exchanges, with a hit of apparently lazy ease.

The arm is the nearest part of the target and it is well to remember that a series of attacks in this area, unsettling the opponent, may create the chances for a sudden switch of direction and a hit elsewhere. Similarly, a threat to the mask may be followed by an attack to the foot and vice versa. Will the opponent be able to change direction? As a game plan the scheme has much to recommend it, but even the most judicious use of the target's extremities cannot always be guaranteed to distract the opponent.

On the rare occasions, when faced with an opponent who follows the blade with orthodox successive parries and against whom attacks and renewals of attack have failed, it may be possible to employ the compound attack with a single feint, or more rarely still, two feints. Such attacks are possible in any line.

It is rather more practicable to make feints in the high line to induce the opponent to raise his hand, then to attack the knee.

In any such situation the defender must rely on successive parries, which are needed more at *épée* than any other weapon, owing to the multiplicity of the opponent's blade actions. Cultivate a defence pattern moving from the high or medium to the low line, or vice versa, which increases the chance of a successful parry rather than keeping in the same line all the time. Counter of *sixte–octave* is always better than two counters of *sixte*. We hope that we will not be accused of over-subtlety if we suggest that occasionally the real 'thinking' épéeist should take two counters of *sixte* – thus foxing the opponent hoping to deceive counter of *sixte–octave*. Diagonal parries, as we have said, must be handled with care; most effective are those from *sixte* terminating in *prime*.

The more varied the repertoire, the better.

It is not always sufficiently realised how vital it is to seize every opportunity of exploiting *tempo* or time, that is, to launch attacks, counter-attacks, stop-hits, or whatever term is used, on any unguarded action or feint of the adversary. In the early stages of a competition, when ability to concentrate is at its maximum, *tempo* predominates.

Limited fencers, concentrating on what they can do well, can be very successful with stop-hits. Later, as fatigue takes its toll, technique comes into its own. Nevertheless, the fencer of high technical standards should not under-rate *tempo*. At least one authority has asserted that a top-class technician could, by relying exclusively on *tempo*, 'establish absolute domination of the *piste*'.

Unfortunately, genuine exploitation of *tempo* has become confused with the counter-attack designed to force a double hit. This has become all too prevalent at both elementary and international level. Beginners do it because they are too clumsy and ignorant to do otherwise; the world class, because they are exceedingly adroit at seizing any suitable opportunity. In a duel one hit is generally enough; and *épée* fencing was originally intended to reproduce the conditions of the duel. A double hit therefore meant a double defeat. Now it can seal a victory. The rules being what they are, it is perfectly fair to use them to one's advantage; but it is a matter for regret that the multi-hit bout has radically altered the whole character and concept of *épée* fencing.

With regard to preparations: a change of engagement enables an attack to be made from the unexpected side.

For those who favour the *prise-de-fer*, feints can lure the opponent's blade into a position for a bind or *enveloppement*, though the odds are probably against his rising to the bait. Attacks to the body are frequently prepared by a *prise-de-fer*; it is safer, so take this precaution if possible.

Those who cannot avoid the opponent's bind or *enveloppement* at the outset can rely on the ceding parry; if they cannot do this, their best hope is to retire with the greatest alacrity.

The *remise* is either instinctive and immediate, or premeditated, becoming in effect a stop-hit on the riposte. Thus a *remise* to the arm with opposition on the recovery will deflect a riposte to the outer arm.

Against the opponent who closes the measure and persists with renewals of attacks, retreat, leaving the point in line, maintain a straight arm and keep the adversary at a distance.

If contemplating counter-time, see how the opponent reacts to feints. If he is inclined to stop-hit, go for counter-time. Perhaps he is orthodox and parry-ripostes; then it may be that here is one of the rare opportunities for a counter-riposte.

Various Types of Fencers

This section is included for convenience and quick reference, although the ground has been well covered in the past.

The straight arm fencer Some few may still be encountered who maintain a perfectly straight line from shoulder to point. Use angular attacks or feints at arm out of distance to establish the system of his defence, but beware of a sudden *flèche*. Conversely, eschew the straight-arm guard when the opponent is strong in angular attacks and *prises-de-fer*. Withdraw the arm and rely on the parry-riposte and unexpected stop-hit, or learn to cede with the parry, leaving the point in line with the body, a wider target which reduces the danger of missing.

Suggestions have been made that, to deceive an attacker, the extended arm and plenty of stop-hits should be used against feints and false attacks if one's real preference is for defence with orthodox parries. One reverts to standard practice when one is satisfied that the opponent, doomed to discomfiture, fancies that he has analysed one's style. We question the wisdom of putting oneself in an unaccustomed position where the procedures are unfamiliar. It is possible to over-elaborate.

The bent arm guard   This is more extreme than the orthodox position described in the first section of this book. These fencers usually employ variations of foil parries. The raising and lowering of the blade to parry takes longer than the slight movement of the point with the fully extended arm. So, attack the extremities, e.g., feint at the mask and hit the leg, or vice versa. If employing this guard for any reason, a parry of *seconde* and riposte high is feasible if there is enough time without conceding a double hit.

Tall and Short   That master who first advised a careful study of the opponent's physique made a strong point. The short fencer, contrary to popular belief, is not necessarily quicker and more adroit at close quarters; yet he must endeavour to get inside his loftier opponent's distance safely – then and then only has he the advantage, as the tall fencer finds that his accustomed distance has gone.

Clearly, therefore, the shorter fencer must be prevented from getting within one's distance, by constant angulated attacks at his wrist and forearm. Avoid attacking the body – this forfeits the natural advantage of superior height and reach.

Against **the fencer of superior speed**, the distance is all important. Repeated changes of relative blade position, in varying speed, will disrupt the rhythm of his attacks.

The beater and **taker of the blade**   The answer here is either complete evasion of his weapon or the ceding *dérobement*. Don't allow him to gain control of your blade, but, keeping the arm well forward, disengage.

The ex-foilist frequently withdraws his hand and arm when parrying. Following a false attack, he is extremely vulnerable to a *redoublement en flèche* to hand or shoulder. If while recovering to guard, he bends his arm to parry the riposte, riposte indirectly.

The 'foilist-épéeist' fences at high speed at relatively close measure, using much of the repertoire of classical foil, such as engagements and their change, counter-ripostes and the like. Do not concede the initiative by indulging in fancy sword-play at close quarters – fence *épée*, not the style he wishes to impose.

The *flècheur* Stop-hit immediately, retire or close the distance. The circular parry, held until the opponent's blade is past, is very well; but at *épée* lifted *septime* is almost as effective as *prime*. Both leave a margin of time to score with a riposte. Either give no ground at all and stand up to the attack, or step back.

From **the ultra-defensive, patient type**, draw a stop-hit, and riposte following a *prise-de-fer* (if that is possible). False attacks at his wrist facilitate a *redoublement* by disengagement. Nor does this type of fencer relish the combat being forced on him at close quarters.

The low-line attacker Those favouring this tactic frequently fall forward, lowing the sword-arm, and are asking for a stop-hit anywhere on the upper target. A variant of this type is *the croucher*, holding the sword-arm well back and low, specialising in low-line attacks, pecks at the hand, and preferring stop-hits to parries. The answers are: keep the hand out of reach, and parry *octave* which further exposes his already vulnerable upper target. Threats to the face should make him stand up. Any *flèche* from this sort of fencer is bound to be slow off the mark and begging for a stop-hit; alternatively, parry and take a *prise-de-fer*.

Some fencers cultivate **an open guard** with the blade out of reach, but carrying the disconcerting threat of angulated attacks and stop-hits. If they are inclined to parry, resort to compound attacks at widely separated parts of the target; if they prefer to stop-hit, counter-time is the obvious solution.

An extreme example of this type used to be known as the fly-fisherman and it is possible that a rare survivor of the breed may still be encountered. His *en garde* position was like an ungainly sack of potatoes, his weapon held aloft to one side as though about to make a cast. Rely on speed, distance, and direct attacks. Counter-time is none too easy, because of the bewildering variety of angles from which the counter-attack may come.

Lastly, there is **the bouncer**, perpetually leaping up and down during an entire bout. Peter Jacob exploited this with immense success in the 'sixties. The idea is to distract your opponent and increase mobility for the *flèche* with which Jacob scored the majority of his hits. Refuse to be distracted or to lose concentration; above all, refrain from following the movement up and down with your eyes.

11: Against the Left-hander

When facing the left-hander, keep the point as well as the hand well out to *sixte* to profit from the protection of the whole blade. When on the offensive, repeated threats in *sixte* may open the left-hander's *quarte* line by provoking an exaggerated degree of covering. The opposite can also be true. Making the left-hander uncertain about his safety in *quarte* may reduce his vigilance in *sixte* – and the outside lines are those where the left hander is vulnerable.

A high feint or false attack to the upper target, causing the opponent to raise the sword-arm, can be followed by a hit or *redoublement* to the knee.

The *quarte-croisé* riposte, difficult against a fencer of the same hand, dominates the left-hander's blade and works if he leaves his arm straight. Keep the hand well out to *quarte*. However, the time-hit by *sixte-croisé* or counter of *sixte-croisé* are both more effective.

The left-hander will have been told exactly the same things. The defence against his *croisé* of *sixte* must be the ceding parry of *quarte*, pronated *tierce* (low) or opposition *octave*. Full marks if the *croisé* can be prevented altogether by a stop-hit beforehand!

Like all stop-hitters, the left-handed specimen should be met with counter-time, using parries and *prises-de-fer*.

Left-handed angulated attacks are countered in exactly the same way as those of a right-hander – namely, by use of the *coquille*. It is a matter of the 'mirror-opposite'!

The left-hander's beat-attack is generally at the outside or top of the arm. Exaggerate the covering in *sixte* with a slight raising of the hand, and stop-hit beneath the adversary's hand.

Those left-handers who *flèche* into *quarte* should be parried in *prime* or lifted *septime*. Should they attack on the outside of the defender's blade, a *croisé* of *septime*, with the sword-hand in the lifted position is viable; but a speedy attack will arrive before the *croisé* is completed. The alternative is a counter of *quarte* in the line of *sixte* – the contraction parry.

The amount of ground yielded, if any, will depend on circumstances, but a step back when parrying the *flèche* is a precautionary measure and may boost the sense of confidence.

For **Counter-action** and **Contraction** parries. See *Against the left-handed foilist* (p. 41).

Part Four
SABRE

1: Attacks

NB: In view of recent rule changes see Appendix V

The success of an attack depends very largely on its being delivered from the correct distance. Distance is not merely relative to the opponent; it relates to what one does or intends to do, and whether the opponent reacts in the way desired. He may fail to do so; but as long as the appropriate distance has been maintained, nothing has been lost.

Today two conflicting schools of thought have emerged. One side advocates an exaggeratedly long distance, from which a minimum of three foot actions is needed to reach the opponent. At the other extreme, the distance is so greatly reduced before any attack that the latter inevitably consists of a single blade action which can hardly be avoided.

It seems that some supporters of the long distance advocate that the sword-arm should not be straightened until half-way through the *flèche*. Sixty years ago, the Spanish master Castello suggested that feints should be made with a half-extended arm, thus facilitating the parry of any stop-cut. More recently, it has been recommended that the arm should be half-straightened on the first feint, three-quarters on the second, fully with the cut. Admirable in theory, but in practice mechanical reflex actions would prevent it.

There is one serious disadvantage in all this. The *flècheur* will indeed parry a simple stop-cut, which is probably the idea of the bent arm, but is dangerously vulnerable to a compound counter-attack.

As for the close-quarter method, it is at once the cause and effect of double attacks, there being only time to think of one thing. It is unnecessary to comment on this devaluation of a magnificent weapon.

Some authorities have specified in precise detail the part of the blade to be used when making a cut, going as far as to prescribe the top two centimetres or three inches. There is no need to be as precise as this. Any part of the fore-edge can be used, but for one's own safety cuts shoʉld be made with the minimum amount of blade commensurate with an effective hit.

It is estimated that at sabre over eighty per cent of successful attacks are simple, whether starting within or out of distance. Nevertheless, they are easier to parry than compound attacks, so may, as a precaution, be executed with a lunge, as it is essential for the attacker to rebound swiftly to the *en garde* position.

Too often the contemporary sabre lunge is little more than a large step and a drag of the rear foot. In contrast, the short, powerful lunge with the body upright to facilitate the parry of a riposte, particularly to the head, is of great value, especially as a counter-attack, when above all the executant must have complete body control in case of a parry.

When attacking the advanced target, use a short lunge; when attacking the body, a preliminary step will be needed. If out of distance, a *flèche* will in the majority of cases have to be employed, particularly when attacking the body.

Attacks at the Arm   If the distance is maintained, attacks can always be made to the arm; if the body is the target, the distance must be changed. In fact, direct attacks at the arm seldom score, other than on an uncovered feint. The majority of hits arriving on the advanced target are the result of compound attacks, stop-hits, or ripostes.

Inside arm and the underside can both be attacked with the back edge. Unfortunately, very few *sabreurs* today can use the back-edge – though mastery of its use would certainly improve their performance – and most rely perforce on the fore-edge, consoling themselves with the fact that the upward cut with the back-edge does expose one's own arm.

Cut at flank   The hand may be slightly lowered, with the point somewhat higher than the hand, to get the right angle for the upward direction.

Cut at head   The fashion now is to defy the traditional rule of keeping the sword-hand down, and deliberately raise it to deliver the cut almost on the back of the head. Others before now have lifted the hand as the cut is completed to get over an insufficient parry of *quinte*. There is some reason for all this, but it tends to be over-exaggerated, and is clearly open to a stop-cut unless executed at very close quarters.

Cut at chest can be delivered by the *molinello*, i.e., the diagonal slicing attack, its circular action being continued with the follow through, as a defence against ripostes at flank or chest. It is most effective *en flèche*. There is a widespread tendency to snatch with this attack and to withdraw the sword-arm too soon, thus missing the target altogether. Those so affected should rely on the alternative and technically orthodox form of attack, with a straight arm, wrist-and-fingers technique, remembering that the 'chest starts at the shoulder' and aiming at the top of the shoulder. The 'slicer' comes into its own as a riposte from *tierce* when it seems to be more natural. The wrist only should be used for the actual cut.

The point Few *sabreurs* now use the point; they are generally either too close or too far away. Nevertheless, it might still enjoy a slight preference over the edge for, in the traditional phase, 'the point is quicker'. It has also been argued that a point attack is less susceptible to a stop-cut at the arm. The hand should of course be pronated and the blade angulated towards the body. The hand should certainly not be higher than when cutting; on the contrary, it should be lowered, remembering that a stop-hit on a simple point action cannot be valid, unless the action is executed very badly indeed.

Indirect Attacks

There has always been confusion and argument about what constitutes an indirect attack at sabre. This is because of the longer sabre measure and the universal absence of blade, so that what in theory are disengagements and cut-overs are unrecognisable as such and in practice become straightforward direct attacks. It is best to say that at sabre indirect attacks pass from one blade line into another.

'Real' indirect actions exist only as ripostes (virtually always the cut-over) or as the end product of a compound attack, or if the fencing has come to very close quarters.

Compound Attacks

Unlike foil and *épée*, both single-plane weapons, sabre must be three-dimensional; cuts can be downwards, upwards, diagonal or across. Hence compound attacks offer a greater chance of success. Like simple attacks, they may start in or out of distance and may be preceded by foot actions but, by sheer force of logic, the final action must always be simple and the aim must be to finish on the open side, i.e., not necessarily the *quarte* side, but the side of the target that is finally left open.

Most compound attacks are executed *en flèche*, but a higher proportion should be made with a lunge, plus a preliminary step if attacking the body.

The cadence of sabre, or the sabre rhythm, can be used to great effect, with subtle changes of time and rhythm by feet, hand and blade. It inadvisable to over-theorise and alternate the long-short cadence (a feint to draw the parry followed by the attack) with the long-short-short of a two feint attack, and then become very clever and attack with a short-long-short to bluff the opponent into supposing that the attack is a badly executed one-feint and forming his parry on the second feint. Enough to say that feints should be deep but quick.

It is also possible to fall back to a parry from a feint. We dislike the term 'broken time' at sabre, we prefer to call it a species of counter-time, to find the opponent's reaction, which may be to retreat or to counter-attack. It may also elicit what parries the opponent prefers.

Considerations of distance will normally require a two-feint attack to be made advancing, each feint accompanied by a step, in principle very short and quick, but subject to modification for the reasons given above.

Occasionally *sabreurs* are encountered who react to every feint, or who only half-react and rely on anticipating the final line of the attack. Against such a one, three-feint attacks are perfectly in order. That the final feint is vital and should be long to fix the opponent's parry is something of a gloss and its value is likely to be more theoretical than real.

Castello has urged that in practice bouts and lessons the number of feints should be increased almost *ad infinitum*. This certainly promotes confident technique, but in competitions feints should be kept to a prudent minimum and never multiplied unduly against the novice *sabreur*, who is apt to panic and suddenly lash out with possibly painful results, or even parry, when least expected.

The type of compound attack should be governed by the opponent's preferred parries, so do not attack blindly with, for example, head-flank, greatly over-done by both fencers and coaches, although it is virtually an attack into a closed line.

Any attack that finishes at chest has the look of a winner; coming from the outside to the inside line, it has less chance of being picked up by a parry.

Without any pretence of exhausting all possible combinations, the following examples would repay study:

Flank-chest
Cheek-chest
Head-chest
Flank-head
Flank-chest-flank
Chest-flank-chest
Chest-head-chest

Compound attacks involving the use of the point have been decried or

PLATE 11   Warming up for the Welsh Open Championship, 1993

PLATE 12 A left–handed *flèche*; Cuomo (left) of Italy and Sandegren (Sweden) in the Men's *Epée* at the Martini Championships 1991

PLATE 13   Double *touche*: Martini 1994, Mazzoni (left) and Pantano (right), both from Italy

PLATE 14   *Quinte* at *épée*: Borrmann of Germany (left) and Cuomo (Italy), Martini finals 1989

extolled by masters of equal standing. However, a feint with the point is tipped to gain a reaction, if only because of its unsettling effect, most *sabreurs* not being used to it.

Feint-point, cut, takes much practice to do well.
Feint-cut, point, is easier and more effective.
A one-two with the point, to the hand. When they drop the weapon with a howl, everyone knows that they have been hit.
A one-two-three with the point aimed at the wrist, either to the inside or outside to suit the situation.

Hard work on these will pay dividends, for most *sabreurs* lack this required technique.
Finally, a real collector's piece:
Flank-chest-head, all with the point.
It at least has the merit of scarcity value.

2: Parries and Ripostes

When parrying at sabre, place the blade. Don't anticipate the parry by moving the weapon into the attack; the riposte will be cleaner. A step back with any parry gives added defence and distance for the riposte. It was once almost compulsory to break ground with 'St George's parry' (*quinte*) and is still helpful with this parry, with which many fencers lack confidence; but in no case should a general principle become automatic.

Most sabre books at some time refer to the two defensive triangles. *Quinte* is common to both; *tierce* and *quarte,* in both of which the point must be a little out of line so that the attack cannot be forced through, are the best protection against lateral cuts, while *prime* and *seconde* are more effective against cuts in a diagonal or near vertical plane. The theory stills holds, though constant repetition in lessons is needed to anticipate the angle correctly. Especially is this true in the selection of either *prime* or *quarte* against the cut at chest. All sabre parries can be 'paired', laterally, horizontally, vertically, e.g., *quarte* and *tierce, prime* and *seconde. Quinte* is followed most readily by *prime* or *seconde,* but also *tierce* or even *quarte.*

The sabre is a three-dimensional weapon, and far more than at the other weapons, every parry is closely related to a riposte which in turn is adjusted to the opponent. The riposte should be a natural reflex action, but nevertheless controllable.

Prime   In high *prime* the hand should be sufficiently high to be able to see under it. From this position the direct riposte is with the back edge to whatever part of the opponent's body that is available. The hand can be lowered to facilitate a premeditated riposte; all will depend on the height of the attacking blade. The hand should be high for a lateral riposte, lower for a premeditated cut-over to the head or chest. If the 'belly cut' is used, ensure that the hand and forearm do not travel across one's body.

Many coaching manuals show the blade in *prime* at forty-five degrees to the ground; one or two not far from horizontal. This is extreme. It remains dismally true that a lateral cut can arrive beneath a *prime* angulated too far forward. Depending on circumstances, there is little harm in the blade being all but vertical, though classically speaking the point should of course be slightly leading.

Seconde   The blade should be in a straight line ahead, point at the height of one's knee. *Seconde* certainly has the merit of gathering in the attacking blade and is as effective against a point attack as a counter of *tierce*, but, if the attack is wide take *prime* and riposte to head.

The most immediate and quickest riposte from *seconde* is not to cheek as is often stated, but with the point to the body; a point disengagement high is equally effective.

Those *sabreurs* who favour a guard position in *seconde* need not hesitate to parry counter of *seconde* against a point attack.

Tierce   Use the fingers and wrist to manipulate the weapon, let the weapon float in the hand which, depending on the height of the attack, can be even lower than in the *en garde* position. A low *tierce* fully protects the outside line, but against a cut at cheek the older and largely discontinued parry of high *tierce* may be used. Even here, the hand should be at most breast high, the blade and forearm forming a straight line.

It has been pointed out many times that the direct riposte *tierce*-head is relatively easy to parry in *quinte*. Instead, try the cut-over to cheek, executed with a lifting of the point. When riposting to the left cheek, use the fore-edge to guard against a counter riposte. The use of the back edge in this case can only be justified if the fencing is at close quarters.

Counter of Tierce   Use the wrist against the point attack, but against cuts rotate the forearm for added strength, especially if the opponent is known to be of the aggressive type. This parry is invaluable against point attacks and beat-cut at chest with the back-edge. Against a sudden attack at chest it is necessary to fall back to *tierce* initially, then take the counter parry and riposte to the open side of the target. Both counter of *tierce* and counter of *quarte* should be accompanied with a step back against a *flèche* attack.

Counter of *tierce* will collect and hold the opponent's blade and is the only sabre parry with enough strength to be made with opposition. This and counter of *quarte* both allow a riposte which could resemble an opposition riposte.

The most deadly example, however, is counter of *tierce*, followed by the lateral cut to the belly; there is nothing much that the opponent can do about this.

Whether *quarte* should be high or low should depend on the height of the attacking blade; either way, your blade should be as vertical as possible. When riposting to cheek, it is better to pronate with a turn of the wrist and cut with the fore-edge than to attempt a back-edge cut, despite the allegedly greater speed of this alternative. For *quarte* cut-over flank the fore-edge should again generally be used.

Counter of *quarte* is essential if the opponent's blade is on the inside.

At close quarters, *tierce* and *quarte* are the best option; *prime* and *seconde* come into their own at the normal measure and of course are then a 'must' against vertical or diagonal attacks.

Quinte In the controversy between the 'point up' and 'point down' schools, we unhesitatingly support the former, deeming the latter to be a distinct fault. However, the point should not be right up, but only slightly higher than the hand, just sufficient to allow the attacking blade to slide down into the *forte*. Too much lift, and an angulated attack will pass under the blade and score every time. Avoid raising the hand itself too high, but parry forward, about the width of a hand in front of the head. To speed things up, lead in with the body and keep the arm bent.

To make the direct riposte to flank 'sit well down', and drop the sword-hand; but if the opponent has a markedly swift recovery to *tierce*, riposte by cut-over to head.

When facing a *reprise* action, *quinte* or *prime* are the best defences.

Just as with *seconde*, *tierce* and *quarte*, a point riposte from *quinte* is a more than valid option.

Counter of *quinte* (clockwise) was popular in prehistoric times, but is too slow today. Nevertheless, if one is unwary enough to be caught in *quinte* with the opponent's blade on the inside, it must be attempted.

The glamorous but antiquated parry of *sixte* is now coming into its own again, more especially following a parry or position in *tierce*. Properly executed, it appears to catch the opponent's blade with spectacular results. It bears a close resemblance to *quinte*, but the hand, now in supination, is on the left of the fencer's head and well across the body, so that it is possible to 'see through' the parry. The point is slightly up, the blade at right angles to the line of the attack. Rather surprisingly, the riposte by cut-over to flank is found to be as quick or quicker than the direct cut at chest.

Delayed Ripostes

Do not attempt a delayed riposte on the opponent's recovery; the modern *sabreur* will not incur the risk of wasting time trying to find the blade. A delayed riposte is only feasible when retreating. It exploits the opponent's natural reaction parry and can be made into any open line.

Sabre parries are so closely paired that a separate section on successive parries is unnecessary, though one or two observations are relevant.

Prime-seconde. This needs a good pull with the little finger for a strong, firm parry.

Tierce-prime will not be of much use at close range, it should be *tierce-quarte* and hope for the best.

Quinte-tierce, so it is argued, offers fuller protection than *quinte-seconde*. To a great extent, true; but to a low upward cut *seconde* must be the answer.

Quinte-seconde-prime, to a high feint and threats to the opposite sides of the target, is more than hard to do; so as a defence it must be good.

In all cases, open the distance whenever possible.

Ignore all the books which tell you to take half-parries only to feints and wait for the opponent to finish the attack in the predetermined line. Such a system is only suitable for a professional fortune teller; the only sane policy is to parry properly each time, or not to move the blade at all until the final movement.

Ripostes at Arm

The arm is a difficult target, moving all the time and the opponent will endeavour to try and not show too much of it. But against a quick recoverer to guard, go for it with a detached parry and an angulated blade.

Indirect and Compound Ripostes

We shall not add to what we have said already about indirect blade actions in relation to the various parries; there is not the same clear distinction between direct and indirect actions at sabre as there is at foil.

Compound ripostes, however, cannot go entirely unmentioned, even though they are a rarity today, modern sabre being far more direct, more instant; two-feint ripostes are virtually impossible, there simply is not the time and they may safely be ignored.

Compound ripostes should be co-ordinated with the reactions of the opponent, and may be made after a slight pause, more especially when on the retreat from a *flèche*. Feints may be suggested by a menacing angulation of the edge, or indeed with any movement of head or body which could influence the action at the other end.

It may be found that compound ripostes really occur when the attacker recovers with an instinctive parry of *tierce*, as most do in England, and ought not, as it leaves them vulnerable against a cut-over to chest-flank.

This brings us back to a point already made – namely, that against an opponent quick to recover in *tierce*, the riposte from *quinte* should go to head rather than flank. Logically, therefore, a compound riposte should be head-flank if the opponent is fast in falling back to *tierce*, flank-head if he is slow. This is valid enough in the abstract, but it is feared that there will be disappointments in its operation.

Counter-Ripostes

Before a counter-riposte can even be considered, the riposte must first be parried. By long practice a defensive reflex can be cultivated and it is better not to snatch the blade automatically back to *tierce*. That makes it harder to parry the cut at chest, and in any case the eye has its part to play. All this must be practised on the lunge, during and after recovery, and while going forward.

Counter-ripostes are generally instinctive but can be pre-meditated; it all depends on the fencer's brain and training. They generally occur at close quarters, so the edge rather than the point comes into play. Generally speaking, the first counter-riposte will be executed *en flèche*, e.g., beat-cheek, then *tierce*-head or *quarte*-cheek.

Certain great Hungarian *sabreurs* have been known to execute five or six counter-ripostes, but such virtuosity is uncommon and although good masters will give routine lessons in which seven or eight are reached, the second counter-riposte is about the most that can realistically be hoped for in a bout; and then it will most probably be with mobility on the retreat from a *flècheur*.

One or two examples will suffice:

Quinte-chest, *seconde*-cheek
Quinte-head, *quinte*-head

In the latter example, revert to *tierce* before the second parry. In this case, an instant return to *tierce* is justifiable, so many fencers automatically delivering their counter-riposte to flank after parrying *quinte* to a riposte.

3: Counter-attacks, Stop-hits and Stop-cuts

Counter-attacks may be performed against almost any movement which is executed slowly or with inferior techniques; more especially against compound attacks with a step forward, *en flèche*, or in two-time.

Compound counter-attacks, even with two feints, may occasionally be successful on the opponent's preparation, and to precede them with attacks on the blade is a useful precaution.

It is essential to be ready to step or spring back, especially after a stop-cut. Lean forward and cut as the rear leg is withdrawn; parry as the leading leg follows it. A great leap back – *salto in dietro* the Italians call it – obviates the need for the parry but puts one out of distance. It is undesirable to execute stop-cuts with an advance, let alone a *balestra*. A dangerous collision becomes all too likely.

Although most stop-cuts are made at the arm, the rest of the body should not be neglected.

The back edge of the sabre can be used against the inner arm; *prime* follows, an effective but difficult action which has to be ingrained and needs great control. It should be unnecessary to state that should the fore-edge be used against this part of the target, the blade must be appropriately angulated.

A stop-cut underneath the arm on a badly executed feint or attack at head is always satisfying; whether the fore- or back-edge is used in this case depends entirely on the preference of each fencer.

In the *salle*, in co-operation with a colleague, repeated stop-cuts should be sedulously practised – at one point, at two points (e.g., forearm and upper arm), then all round the target, then in the reverse direction. Finally, try to alternate the cuts with point hits. This sounds easy enough, but it is surprising how often it breaks down in practice.

The old stop-cut, parry-riposte exercise is as valuable as ever. Start with one 'triangle' e.g., outer-arm *tierce*-head, inner arm *quarte*-cheek, underneath *quinte*-flank, then add on the stop-cuts, parries and ripostes for *prime, seconde* and *quinte* once more. At an agreed stage add steps forward and backwards on each parry. Finally the riposte can be made with a lunge.

Stop-hits with the point, especially on compound attacks executed *en flèche* or with a step forward, were once very popular and effective but are unwise today, as few presidents would award the desired priority.

We append a few examples which some *sabreurs* may wish or care to practise to help improve their all-round efficiency; one or two are highly complex and although theoretically possible, direct action is generally the key to success today.

1   On the opponent's attempt to take or attack the blade in *quarte*, disengage with a feint of a cut, disengage again with the point.

2   On the opponent's feint of cut, beat and disengage with the point, or beat, cut to head.

3   On the opponent's advance in *tierce* or with a feint at head, counter-attack with the point from the *en garde* position or with a lunge or *flèche* according to the distance.

4   On the opponent's advance with an attempt to take the blade in *seconde*, disengage to the chest either with the point or stop-cut.

5   On the opponent's attack, parry *quinte*, riposte flank, or stop-cut, *quinte-*flank, according to whether his arm is straight or bent.

4: Preparations of Attack

Footwork

The cross over (similar to a light fast run) is more frequently employed at sabre than at the other weapons. It is often combined with an ordinary step or *balestra* preceding a lunge or *flèche*. The head and body should be kept upright. The rear foot should land with the toe pointing forward as the heel is grounded; it then swivels to resume its normal *en garde* position. When using the cross over in retreat do not worry too much over the exact placing of the feet. The sole object is to get out of the way as soon as possible.

We have mentioned earlier that the sabre lunge sometimes resembles something between a step and a half lunge. One should either step or lunge. Remember that the sabre lunge is shorter than the foil lunge, so that it is easier to *flèche* as a *reprise* from this position.

Both steps and *balestras* should be varied as preparations for the attack, whether by lunge or *flèche*. Rapid short steps are the norm, but steps must never become mechanical, and distance must always be modified in relation-ship to the circumstances and the particular opponent.

Following an initial step forward, a step back, or half a step back, paradoxi-cally will give added momentum to a *flèche*. Some masters even advocate one step forward and then two back before the *flèche* with a compound blade action. In our opinion 'you pays your money and you takes your choice'. In other words, you should suit the action to the current situation.

Beats

A beat with contact of the medium part of the blade to 'break the attack' may be made as the opponent is feinting or preparing an attack with a step forward – if you are good enough to do it.

At one time most Continental presidents distinguished between beats on the *foible* which they accepted as a valid attack with right of way, and beats on the *forte* which, they argued, would not have deflected the blade. Hence, in the latter case a riposte off the beat would have right of way.

Today it would seem that a beat can either give you right of way for your attack, or it is sometimes read as an attack which is parried. It seems that today most presidents do not use their ears so are unable to tell the difference between an attack on the *foible* of a blade, or the beat that arrives on the *forte*.

There is a distinct difference between the two; if one trains one's ears, one is able to tell the difference.

The beat will certainly speed up any attack. While executing the beat the arm may be slightly extended to increase the reach, but otherwise should move as little as possible and the blade, carefully controlled, should rebound into the line of the feint or attack. Use the forearm and the front edge for a firm strong beat that should open the line.

Discard any notion of a moderate beat seeking a reaction. Most *sabreurs* will endeavour to ignore attacks on the blade. On the other hand, a change-beat into *quarte* may be executed with the back-edge for the sake of speed and convenience.

A beat with the back-edge underneath the opponent's blade followed by a cut to head is difficult but viable.

Beats are excellent preparations for compound attacks. The following exercises involving the beat can be extremely useful:

1   On the opponent's beat, answer the beat, cut to cheek.

2   On the opponent's change-beat answer the beat, cut to head.

3   On the opponent's beat inside the blade, change beat, cut to head, cheek, chest.

All the above exercises can and should be practised with all the foot actions that one is able to use.

PLATE 15 (left) Who hit who? Khun (Switzerland) (left) and Leroux (France) in the 1989 Martini Championships

(below) A good left-handed *flèche*: Srecki of France (right) in the 1989 Martini Men's *Epée*

PLATE 16   Athletic? The Martini 1991 Men's *Epée* with Rivas of Columbia (left) and Srecki (France)

5: Renewals of Attack

Remise

In our opinion there can be no such thing in modern sabre. Either the opponents hold the parry, or scuttle back at high speed, in which case the *remise* would meet empty air.

Redoublements

The redouble can be premeditated against badly executed indirect or compound ripostes, though chance is likely to pay a major part in the matter. When opportunity serves, redouble to any part of the target that is open. It is easy to redouble after the opponent's parry of *quinte* – everything is exposed – but beware of the direct riposte. Following a *redoublement* by an opponent attempting a cut at chest, *prime* is the best parry to take.

It has been noted that the fencer who just leans back with his parry instead of stepping back, is more vulnerable to the *redoublement*. This may be true, but the tendency today is to break away to a safe distance, rather than relying on the withdrawal of the body. It is a 'must' to get out of distance of the *redoublement*, whether it be by an attack or riposte. The use of the point is highly unlikely in any of the above cases. However, many renewals are preceded by a beat or a compound attack accompanied, if needed by the distance, a *balestra* or *flèche*.

The *redoublement* of the riposte is often automatic. One example, simple in theory, but which needs great speed in its execution is the *redoublement* to flank following a parry of *quinte* and riposte under the arm. One of the few times that the flank is really open.

Reprise

A beat may precede or accompany the *reprise*, a slight bending of the sword-arm being allowable to effect it. A *reprise en flèche* with a compound blade action is often the surest way of gaining a hit. Even the most skilful of *sabreurs* is less certain against a sudden renewal of attack with one, or better still, two feints.

A *reprise* following a recovery backwards at sabre is so rare as not to merit discussion; but that one is possible we will not deny.

The defence against renewals

By far the best defence is two or more parries. Against the renewal of the attack on one's preparation, they are essential. But there will generally be a slight pause between the two parries which, properly exploited, allows an alternative course of action. For example, against the opponent's beat attack, parry *seconde* and pause – then parry *prime* to the *redoublement* and riposte to the head. If there is no *redoublement* riposte *en flèche*.

The pause can be turned to advantage following the parry of a riposte as well as the parry of an attack. Hold the parry of your opponent's riposte, and *flèche* if there is no renewal. If there is, make the second parry and then *flèche*.

6: The *Dérobement*

The *dérobement* should be used against the opponent trying to advance with a blade preparation; here, the use of the point does seem more natural, and in some cases comes into its own.

The *dérobement* may also be used against the opponent playing for counter-time; for example, on the opponent's attempt to take the blade in *tierce*, give him the stop-point by disengagement, then deceive his parry with a cut to cheek.

7: Broken Time

Despite our earlier observations, Broken Time can play a part in sabre. The attack may be delivered in two-time with a pause in the middle; or again, there may be a pause before the final action of a compound riposte, though in this case it is essential to be very certain of the opponent's reaction. The step forward, step back and *flèche* (see *Preparations* pp. 71–72) also has the effect of provoking an incorrect or premature reaction from the opponent.

Further examples:

1 Cut at chest and deliberately miss, attack to chest *en flèche*.

2 Feint at chest, pause, cut at chest. The feint and the 'slicing' action should be executed with the hand in pronation.

3 Feint at head, pause, cut at head.

4 Feint at head with a short lunge, bring up rear foot and *flèche* at head.

On the last three examples, the arm should be slightly bent on the feint so that the opponent does not find the blade.

8: Counter-time and Second Intention

With regard to **second intention** as opposed to pure counter-time, bear in mind that there is at least the possibility of a pre-meditated counter-riposte. Draw the riposte and deliver both the parry and counter-riposte *en flèche*. This must, however, be regarded as only occasionally possible, depending on the skill of the executant and still more on the chances of involuntary co-operation on the part of the opponent. Classic examples of an attack with a lunge, then a parry and counter-riposte on the lunge, valid until the advent of the electric sabre, will not work now. The changed concept of distance (either very close or exaggeratedly far apart) renders it exceedingly difficult to anticipate the correct distance for the counter-riposte.

To parry *prime* while on the lunge, as suggested in certain old textbook examples, is impossible at any weapon, above all at sabre. Low or high *prime* may be taken against a *flèche* or even a lunge attack, but never on the lunge.

In theory **counter-time** is perfectly permissible, but it plays far less part in sabre than used to be the case. The modern *sabreur* gives insufficient thought to tactics, and tends to accept any momentary situation without consideration of what his opponent may be going to do. Many contemporaries have no idea of making feints to draw stop-hits. Their idea of a feint is to try and hit.

Moreover, the instinctive reaction today is to parry and riposte rather than to stop-hit; and what is more, if and when a counter-attack does come, it will not necessarily be made to the arm as used so often to be the case.

Observation and a reasonable degree of certainty are needed if a required action is to be drawn from an opponent and then exploited. It is impossible to know exactly what is in an opponent's mind, but one can try and anticipate his instinctive or controlled reflex. **That is counter-time.**

There are two important principles which must never be forgotten and form the basis of all counter-time. First, the bait (or action) must appear to be authentic. Uncovered feints, attacks on the blade or attempts to take it, steps forward, false attacks, body feints, all are serviceable, but must be justified in relation to the opponent and his idiosyncrasies and his previously established reactions. It is no good just making a list of every possible example and then trying them all in turn.

Secondly, as a general rule and whenever possible, keep it simple. The stop-cut or stop-point is most conveniently parried in *tierce* or *quarte* or, in the latter case *seconde*, and a direct riposte with the edge generally follows. On the other hand, there are cases where counter-time has to include successive parries against experienced and subtle opponents who counter-attack with more than one blade action. Against such a one, there arises the possibility of a compound riposte. But do not get carried away – the experienced *sabreur* may be quietly awaiting the second blade action.

However, fencing involving that degree of observation and foresight is extremely rare today so the general rule stands – avoid over-elaboration. Go for the cut at head *en marchant* as a feint – they fall for it even today.

For what was an excellent example of counter-time, consider the following:

Step forward with a feint at head.
Parry *seconde* to the point counter-attack with a lunge.
Riposte to chest.

There may be a slight lifting of the hand as an extra safeguard when parrying *tierce* to the stop-cut at outer arm. When threatened by the stop-cut to the inner arm, a turn of the guard with a flexing of the wrist is a quicker defence than full *quarte*; but keep awake in case the counter-attack does not come where you expected after all.

If the opponent's reaction, when his counter-attack is parried, is to return to guard covered, an indirect riposte *en flèche* or with a *balestra* is perfectly viable in theory. If indeed the opponent is given to the stop-cut-parry-riposte routine, and better still, steps back with the parry, there is a decent chance of success; not otherwise. Today's *sabreur* is far less technical than his forefathers and does not think as they used to do.

As a defence against the opponent using counter-time, keep one step ahead of him; let him parry the stop-cut, then parry the final movement of his riposte, preferably with a counter-parry. With regard to second intention, as opposed to pure counter time, bear in mind the premeditated counter-riposte. Draw the opponent's riposte, and deliver both the parry and counter-riposte *en flèche*.

9: Tactics

As we have already said, sabre tactics have been affected by the extremes of distance now generally adopted. Hence even more than before, the importance of preparations by false attacks and variations of the length of steps to get inside the opponent's measure. False attacks have always been used to gain distance; then comes the *reprise*.

Those who favour the *redoublement* (with or without an additional foot action) and the *reprise*, should induce their opponents to parry *quinte*. The whole target is then at the attacker's disposal. It may be added here that at sabre a *redoublement* is always a possibility following the parry of the attack, riposte or counter-riposte. When facing a *redoublement*, parry both cuts. When false attacks are being used by the opponent as preparation for a *reprise*, attack on his feint. The *remise* has virtually disappeared altogether from the sabre repertoire.

The use of the counter-attack, whether with the point or edge, has tended to decline of late. In the old days it was not at all uncommon for a stop-cut to be made in the middle of a phrase. But distance is now the criterion – given the correct distance a stop-hit can still be most effective; if it is not exactly right, and in time, you are certain to be hit yourself.

As a protection against a stop-hit on the inside line, counter of *tierce* is by far the most useful.

Remember that the change of cadence at sabre is one of your most useful weapons. Varying the cadence of both foot and hand by alternating the increase or reduction of one's normal speed is one way of attempting to control the bout. Suddenly increase the final movement of a phrase, or change the speed of the attack after a series of false attacks and feints. On the other hand, against an opponent superior in speed, never make the mistake of trying to equal or outdo him. On the contrary, attempt to slow things down by changing the cadence, so as to have the chance to deliver indirect or even compound ripostes with broken time.

Very occasionally, someone may be met who can use the point. He may be an eccentric survivor; or he may have read this book. *Tierce* and *quarte* are not altogether foolproof against the point; *seconde* and counter of *tierce* are much safer.

It has always been said that counter of *tierce*, taken repeatedly, will disrupt the development of fast and tricky compound attacks. This is not to be decried; but make sure the attacks really are compound.

When reasonably certain that the opponent has a taste for compound ripostes, instantly redouble the attack.

Against **the persistent attacker**, rely on your parries and ripostes. This is equally true of attacks that are pressed home with a succession of *balestras* and *flèches*. Rather than try to stop-hit, it is better to step back with more than one parry as an additional precaution. It is inadvisable to shorten the measure as at foil – a cut can still be delivered at very close quarters. On the other hand, don't automatically retire; it may not always be necessary. Retain some freedom of manoeuvre.

The ultra-cautious defensive sabreur Whatever you do, he will not attack, and refuses to respond with the orthodox reactions that you want. You must be equally patient; watch and wait for your opportunity; beat him for speed, go one up and then wait for 'Time' to be called, relying on the parry-riposte, if in desperation he should be driven to attack.

We have already talked of the danger of becoming too complicated against **the novice**; he is too unpredictable. If possible, by means of false attacks and feints establish what parries he prefers, and what his reactions are to your feints; then rely on both speed and technique to beat him with direct attacks. Refuse to react to his feints, most of which will be by instinct, few with deliberate intent. His faulty technique and propensity to bend the sword–arm when attacking or feinting sometimes has the same effect as a deliberate attack with a bent arm.

It also used to be said that novices, being unused to point attacks, were easily upset by them; but in this respect they now differ but little from the majority of their comrades.

We would be very wary of the use of the point against a compound attack either with a step or *flèche*. A stop-hit with the point, though lethal, requires the most expert timing, requiring a high discipline of reflexes and sense of distance.

10: The Left-handed *Sabreur*

One of the most difficult *sabreurs* to cope with. They are never easy to fence against at any weapon. One of the most rewarding ways to record hits on the left-handed fencer, paradoxical though it may seem, and depending to some extent on what parries he prefers, is to attack his outside line, i.e., covered line. Any preparation there will make him open his inside line where he will then be vulnerable. Any beat on his blade either inside or outside may give one the chance to score a hit if he will allow his blade to be found.

Many left-handed fencers prefer to parry *seconde* or *tierce* to nearly everything in which case they can be attacked with indirect actions which either follow or deceive their blade.

For fairly obvious reasons, most left-handed fencers attack the right-hander's arm; some answers are to use counter of *tierce* or *seconde* as a defence pattern and to use the point whenever possible as a riposte.

The fact is, and it would be foolish to try to disguise it, the left-handed *sabreur* is the most awkward of opponents; far more difficult than his counterpart at foil or *épée*. In one respect, he is certainly vulnerable – to stop-hits under the arm, just behind the guard. However, to be certain of having the hit, make sure that you hit but are not hit, or you will find that most presidents will award a hit against you.

For the rest, one is limited to one's own skill and system of defence plus knowledge. Hone your own skills and develop your personal technique to increase your confidence and ability. It would also be an advantage if your master was able to give you a high standard of lessons as a left-handed fencer himself.

Appendix 1

CLOSE-QUARTER FIGHTING

The classical masters had little to say about close-quarter fighting, other than that the distance should be opened again as quickly as possible. It was not until the 'sixties that a combination of the electric weapon and the new aggressive style of fencing brought the matter under serious consideration.

Some fencers adapt well to close-quarter fighting and seem to revel in it. Others are less enthusiastic but must certainly be prepared to defend themselves and if possible also attack if the situation is forced upon them.

The first thing to remember is never to step back. This merely opens the target and exposes it to a thrust as they withdraw. It is not now permissible to take evasive action by means of *in quartata* actions, ducking right down and so forth.

Parries therefore must be executed, albeit with a modified technique. High line parries should be made with the hand lower than normal, those in the low line with the hand higher. This renders the blade more vertical and reduces the chance of hitting off-target at foil. The step-in parry comes into its own and should be made wider than usual and with the point angulated at the opponent's target.

The whole of the opponent's back is vulnerable at close quarters. When your opponent is bending down lower, stand right up. A cut-over riposte from *prime* to the back is one useful option here. A cut-over from *octave* (really a cut – under!) can go to the middle of the back; ripostes from *octave* and *quarte* to the inside target.

Close thrusts, ripostes and *remises* may be with either opposition or angulated. The cut-over is of more service than the disengagement, but more difficult to do, and in these situations, it is advantageous to turn inwards or even to get right alongside the opponent.

Appendix 2

TRAINING EXERCISES

It is impossible to have absolute fitness, but one can be very fit in different ways for different things. We may be very fit as a swimmer, but have a very different level of ability, say, as a footballer, due to the fact that we will have developed a fitness through training that is biased towards the activity that is favoured. For fencing, some parts of the body will require special attention, in particular the muscles of the arms, shoulders, abdomen and back, plus the legs, lungs and heart.

The strength and endurance of the body can be increased through regular exercise (balanced physical activity which should involve the whole body) and also a balanced diet. For overall fitness we need to develop and combine **mobility, strength** and **endurance**, the three factors of prime importance for any fitness training programme, coupled with controlling our weight and stress tolerance.

Mobility is having a full range of movements in all joints, allowing you to be able to twist and turn and bend in any direction, to your maximum ability, passing through a full range of flexion, extension, rotation, abduction and adduction movements. Any system of fitness training should be started with mobility exercises, to help stretch and tone the body up, prior to stamina building, using a system of slow, controlled movements, avoiding any sudden or violent movements which could over stretch and possibly tear muscles. This suppleness, acquired at the beginning of the exercises, allows the body to obtain far better results.

Mobility is most effective if exercising joints is confined to one area at a time. One example of this is Arm Circling, which mobilises the shoulder joints. While the back and head should be kept straight and still, the back should not be allowed to hollow so that the arms can reach further back, as this would defeat the object of the exercise.

Muscular **strength** can be increased by exercising muscles against resistance by either external resistance, e.g., by lifting weights or against body weight. To develop strength, the resistance must be applied progressively, starting with a small number of repetitions and then progressively increasing both them or the weights.

Endurance or **stamina** is concerned with the ability to repeat actions over and over again, or to sustain the muscular contraction.

Any system of exercise that exploits all the factors necessary, i.e., mobility, strength and stamina, should all start off at low levels of repetitions, and be increased in volume and weight progressively, according to the individual's needs. Before starting on a course of training exercises, it may be necessary to improve the general level of fitness and control weight (see Appendices 3 and 4). If you consider yourself seriously unfit and/or overweight it is wise to consult your doctor before embarking on strenuous exercise or strict dieting.

The body will not work at the same pace all the time and everyone has his own body rhythm, that fluctuates during the day. The body also has other rhythms which fluctuate, some over a week, others over a year. These are known as the circadian rhythm; this will determine when your body is at its maximum efficiency, when you feel full of energy and are able to do things more easily than others.

By trying to understand your internal rhythms, you will be able to help yourself to even better fitness. Finding your own daily rhythm will allow you to attempt more commanding things while you are at your most efficient; if you can train at the same time every day, when you are at the peak of your circadian rhythm, the benefits of your training should not only be greater, but the ill effects, if any, should be less.

To maintain fitness, not only do we need to use our muscles by regular exercise, but we need to understand how our minds and emotions will affect our performance under all possible conditions, while also taking into account the indefinable thing that we call stress, which we are subject to in everyday life. However, if exercise is regular and sustained, general fitness will not only bring us a healthy body, but better sleep and possibly a more peaceful state of mind.

Fitness by exercise is divided into the three main groups: mobility, strength and stamina.

Mobility

With the exception of (c) all exercises in the Mobility Section are done with the feet wide apart: (c) should be done with the feet together.

When you have mastered the exercise, start your training programme with five repetitions. When you can do these with comfort, increase the repetitions by the same amount.

A. Arm Circling

With arms at the side, raise both hands from front to rear in a full circle, passing your arms as closely as possible to the ears, in a long slow circular motion. Only the arms should move, the buttocks should be held in and the head should not move. The hips should also be fixed, keeping the trunk from moving backwards and forwards. Breathe in, as the arms go up, and out, as they come down.

B. Side Bends

With the hands on hips, bend sideways first to the left and then to the right, slowly and evenly. The head must stay upright but follow the natural body line, the buttocks should be held in and there should be no movement from below the hips or twisting of the trunk.
Breathe in on one side, and out the other.

C. Trunk: Knee and Hip Bends

Support the body by placing your hands on the back of a chair.
Lower the head towards the left knee, at the same time raising the knee towards the head, then return the leg to the floor and the head to its normal upright position. Repeat the exercise with the right leg. If necessary allow the supporting leg to bend. Do not lift the knee too high. Allow the back to curve first. Aim to reach the forehead with the knee. Allow the head to relax into the knee. When you are strong enough, do the exercise without support. Breathe out as your knee comes up, and in as you recover to the upright position.

D. Head, Arm and Trunk Rotating

Stand with arms extended forward with the palms down at shoulder height. Turn the head, arms, and trunk as far to the left as you can, letting the head lead the body, and allowing the right arm to bend across the body. Repeat to the right, looking as far behind you as possible, without any movement from below the hips. Keep the arms at shoulder level throughout, the buttocks kept in and the back straight, but do not overreach.
Breathe in from one side and out the other.

E. Alternate Ankle Reaching

Place both hands on the left thigh, across the body. Keeping in contact with the leg, reach as far down the leg as possible, return to the upright position and repeat the other side, making sure that the shoulders relax between repetitions. Let the head relax and start the movement first, allowing the back to curve as much as possible. The sideways movement should be as small as possible. If needed, allow the knees to bend to prevent pulling the hamstrings.
Breathe out as you reach downwards and in as you return to the upright position. The exercise should be as continuous as possible.

Strength

Group 1

Stage 1: Stomach

Sit on the edge of a solid chair, hold both sides of the chair with both hands and lean back. Bend both knees to chest and then lower to the ground. Bend the knees as much as possible, keep hold of the chair all the time, do not hurry the movement.
Breathe in as you bring your knees up, out as you lower them.

Stage 2

With the use of support, either people or some kind of weight on the legs, lie on the floor on your back with your arms above your head, roll forward to the sitting position, reaching as far forward as possible, then return to the starting position. Allow the back to curve as much as possible, and if needed bend the knees slightly.
Breathe out as the body curves forward, and in as you return to the original position.

Stage 1: Squats

Place hands on a chair or wall, with the feet 3 in. apart with the heels in and the toes pointing out. Rise up onto the balls of the feet, lower the body by bending the knees, return to the upright position, still on the balls of the feet, lower the heels to the floor. Keep the feet 3 in. apart, back straight, head upright and only bend the knees as far as you are able.
Breathe in as you rise on to the toes, out as you lower to the squat position.

Stage 2

As above but without support and with the feet parallel and hip width apart, with the arms extended as a balance. The heels must now stay flat on the ground throughout while doing parallel squats.
Breathe in as you rise on to the toes, out as you lower to the squat position.

Group 2

Arms: Wall Press Ups
Stage 1
Stand an arm's length from the wall. Place palms of hands on wall, shoulder height with the feet slightly apart. Keep feet flat on floor and allow the elbows to bend until the forehead touches the wall, push back on palms until you return to the original position

Breathe out while the arms are bending, and in while returning to the upright position.

Stage 2
As above but with the arms at waist height, or at the back of a chair or bench. Make sure that the support is secure and firm.

Breathe out while the arms are bending, and in while returning to the upright position.

Back Bends
Stage 1
Lie on your front, place hands on the forehead, lift head allowing the back to bend as far as possible, then lower. Lift the legs as far as possible, then lower, repeat, first head then legs. The feet and legs should stay together. If needed, have someone to give support.

Stage 2
Using a bench, lie over it so that the hips and back are in contact with the bench and your shoulders resting on the floor. Place hands on the head and lift as in stage one. The legs and hips must be held firmly to avoid falling. Keep both hips and legs together.

Breathe in when you lift the head or legs, out when you lower them.

Stamina

Group 3

Stage 1
Running on the Spot
The arms should be loose at the side, do not raise knees too high at first. Aim to get them progressively higher as you increase the time that you are able to maintain.

Stage 2
Bench Steps
Stand in front of a chair or bench, no higher than 18 in., step up on to it with

both feet. After 10 step ups, start with the other foot. Stand up straight on the bench. Place both feet firmly on the floor and bench each time. Aim for a 5 minute exercise, or more.

Strength Exercises with the Use of Weights

Because of the difference in individual physical build, it is not possible to define what weights should be used. This should be decided by the fencer and his or her coach after the first training period. To start with, a weight must be selected that will enable all movements to be learnt and yet thoroughly exercise the participant.

Weights in the range of 15 to 30 lb would be suggested depending upon the individual. You may find these to be very light, but remember that you will have not only to do up to twenty repetitions but also learn the exercise. In later training periods the weights can be adjusted for your own developing strength levels.

When training for strength and power, an exercise should be chosen that will permit five repetitions at the start without loss of present form. As the participant finds it easier to perform the five repetitions, he should increase the number by five, so that he can progress to twenty. When this number is reached, the weight should be increased and so start all over again.

Rest pauses between sets of repetitions should be kept to the minimum. These pauses should only be long enough to permit the breathing to return to normal.

Appendix 3

HEALTH AND FITNESS

When you take exercise the heart will have to beat faster to supply the increased blood supply. If the oxygen intake is inefficient the heart rate will go up very quickly, after even a small amount of exercise. It is of vital importance that the pulse rate is kept within the individual's own degree of fitness.

The pulse at rest for men should be between sixty and eighty beats a minute and between sixty-five and eighty-five for women. This is the rate that the heart has to maintain to supply the body needs when at rest.

In the beginning you may have to rest between exercises to keep your pulse rate down. As fitness improves you will find that you will be able to do more exercise at a lower pulse rate. It is the physiological effort which stimulates training, not the external physical work.

A simple test of general fitness is given below. It is in three levels; Stage One, Level 3, is possibly the lowest that anyone in general health should be at, even if over-weight. In the beginning you may have to rest between exercises and/or the repetitions.

Stage 1

Level 3
Can you walk briskly for up to 3 minutes without shortness of breath?

Level 2
Can you walk briskly for between 3 and 10 minutes without shortness of breath?

Level 1
Can you walk easily for 10 minutes?
Having reached this level just by walking, we can improve this by adding jogging.

Stage 2

Level 1

Walk 50 steps, jog 50 steps per minute, for 6 minutes. If you have to stop before 6 minutes go back to level 1 of the previous exercise.

Stage 3

Level 1

Complete 12 minutes without stopping of Stage 2

If you use the above method, the only limit to your fitness is your own motivation or need. Also, quite the opposite of prevailing notions, older fencers should also be encouraged to take part in the above, as exercise will help to keep joints flexible and muscles more supple and most important of all, help the heart to work better and the body to stay in better condition.

Appendix 4

DIET AND WEIGHT

Your weight is determined by the calories that you put into the body, balanced against the number that you expend. New eating habits will help you to reduce weight; thus, reducing the intake of calories, and greater body activity can increase the output. The two together will help you to reduce weight.

If we attempt to lose weight by walking for example, it is the distance that we traverse that is important and should be the guide, not the speed of the movement. A heavy person will use more calories to walk a mile than will a light person, irrespective of the time taken.

When the fundamental purpose of exercise is to assist in fat reduction, it is preferable to walk at the rate at which the most distance can be covered in comfort. Short bursts of high energy will fatigue the individual before large numbers of calories have been used up and this is relatively ineffective in weight reduction.

Fat loss by exercise is a slow process, especially when the individual maintains an otherwise normal daily life style. This process is usually too slow for most people, because one pound of body weight has the equivalent of 3,500 kilocalories. To produce the energy expenditure of just 500 kilocalories, for anyone unused to heavy or hard exercise, is hard work and will call for a great deal of self-discipline. If one was, shall we say, training by running, this would mean running an extra 5 miles every day.

To attempt fat loss by food alone would also be a severe strain to most people. Again, to lose one pound you must consume 3,500 fewer calories than your body uses. It would take 500 calories fewer each day to lose one pound in a week; this would mean reducing the daily food intake to below about 2,500 calories for a man and 2,000 for a woman with desk jobs.

Rapid weight reduction without exercise or calories restrictions, commonly relies on dehydration, induced by water restrictions, diuresis, or induced sweating, and is temporary. The body needs fluid in copious amounts and the dehydrated individual usually rehydrates within a few days.

Roughly 69% of body weight is water and if one's daily weight fluctuates by more than two pounds, fluid has not been adequately replaced. Such a significant water deficit will compromise any physical performance and even threaten physical fitness and one's general well-being.

One diet rule most doctors and dietitians agree about is the need for fibrous foods and roughage in the daily diet. This roughage, which can be just the wheat husks in wholemeal bread, does two things: it gives something for the muscles of the intestine to push on (because it is not liquefied like processed foods); and it prevents all the water being reabsorbed into the large intestine as the food approaches the end of the alimentary canal. This means that toxic compounds present in food do not stay in the intestines for days or weeks, but are pushed along through the body and got rid of in less than forty-eight hours.

The composition of our diet, i.e., the degree of saturated fats, fibre content, salt, refined sugar etc., will affect our calorie intake. A diet that is inadequate to support the needs of the body, will result in a deterioration in fitness that is needed for exercise.

A substandard diet will cause a reduction in the performance of the physiological systems. The normal intake of fat should not supply more than 45% of the total calories, and the protein and carbohydrate content should be 15% and 65% of the total calories for a day.

Cooking is usually essential for high protein foods particularly meat, peas, and beans. It will help to prepare them for digestion, which is far more difficult in their raw state. Fats, when broken down, produce even more energy, are fairly easy to digest and are little affected by normal cooking.

The following regime should give you the balanced diet which contributes to general fitness; if you stick to the quantities proposed, coupled with regular exercise, you should find that you gradually reduce your weight.

General Rules

- Drink up to 3 pints of water every day (or as much as possible). Water should be the best you can get, bottled, not out of a tap.
- Drink the juice of half a lemon every day (diluted with water if it helps).
- Use only low fat milk in your coffee or tea daily (the water used to make tea or coffee should be in addition to the 3 pints you are drinking every day).
- Before you eat your evening meal, or your last meal of the day, drink at least one pint, or as much as possible of water.
- Cut down on salt, use only wholemeal bread, Ryvita or the like.
- Take a good quality multi-vitamin and multi-mineral pill daily.

- Make your own muesli, using 1 cupful of oats plus 1 tablespoonful of some of the following: all dried fruits, apple, banana, pear, peach, pineapple, prunes, apricot and one tablespoonful of walnuts. In any one week, eat only 4 oz sultanas, 4 oz raisins, 4 eating apples, 4 bananas.
- Use Marmite as often as you like and only non-fat spread.
- Use honey and low fat yoghurt as part of one meal a day.
- In any one week you can eat: 1 green pepper; 3 in. of cucumber; 2 small carrots; 1 sprig of broccoli; 4 large tomatoes; 6 celery sticks; as much watercress and lettuce as you like; 8 small mushrooms; 2 eggs; 4 oz low fat cheese; 4 fish fingers; 8 oz chicken; 4 oz liver; 4 oz tuna; 2 cod steaks

Menus

BREAKFASTS

1. 1 apple, 2 tablespoons of muesli, a small yoghurt.
2. 1 Weetabix, 1 banana, honey, small glass of low fat milk.
3. 1 poached egg, one slice of bread, honey.
4. 1 apple, 2 tablespoons of muesli, 1 Weetabix, honey.
5. 1 slice of bread, honey, small yogurt.
6. 1 apple, 1 Weetabix, honey, small glass of low fat milk.
7. 1 slice of toasted bread, honey, small yogurt.

LUNCHES

1. 1 wholemeal roll filled with watercress, and low fat cheese.
2. 2 slices of toast, honey or cheese, watercress.
3. 2 Weetabix, cheese, watercress.
4. 1 wholemeal roll, watercress, tomato.
5. 2 slices of toast, 1 egg poached.
6. 2 Weetabix, watercress, tomato, cheese.
7. 1 wholemeal roll, cheese, watercress.

EVENING MEAL

1. 2 fish fingers, mushrooms, carrots, Weetabix.
2. Chicken, broccoli, lettuce.
3. 1 egg, mushrooms, carrots, lettuce.
4. 1 cod steak, watercress, tomato.
5. Liver, mushrooms, lettuce.
6. 1 egg omelette, with 2 slices of toast.
7. 1 cod steak, celery, pepper, one slice of toast.

Note: You can eat any of the fruits or muesli with honey or crispbreads at any time if you are hungry.

Appendix 5

THE *FLECHE*

Shortly before going to press, the F.I.E. decreed that at sabre the *flèche* and all foot actions which involved crossing the legs were illegal. However, it seems not impossible that this ruling may yet be rescinded. Therefore, rather than re-write the entire sabre section which would then, in the event of such a repeal, be again inapplicable, we decided to include in this appendix what we hope will provide acceptable and efficient alternatives.

Instead of a *flèche*, precede an attack with:

1 A step or steps
2 A *balestra*
3 A step/steps and *balestra*

The sword-arm may be extended during or after the steps, always with the *balestra*.

When *en flèche* appears in the text, the phrase *en marchant* should generally be substituted.

It should be noted that although a cross-step forward is now illegal, the legs may be crossed in retiring.

GLOSSARY

The majority of our readers are probably fully conversant with fencing terminology. Nevertheless, memory sometimes falters, so the following list, which includes a number of the less commonly used terms, may be useful.

Absence of blade When there is no blade contact on either side.

Academic assault A demonstration bout.

Advance To step forward, to gain ground.

Advanced target The sword-arm at *épée* and sabre.

Angulation To angle the blade with pronation or supination.

Appel A stamp on the floor with the front foot generally preceding an attack.

Assault A bout between two fencers.

Attack An offensive action intending to score a hit on the opponent.

Attacks on the blade Beats, pressures, *froissements, coulés.*

Attacks on the preparation To attack the opponent while he is preparing the way for his attack.

Balestra A short jump forward with both feet preceding an attack.

Barrage A bout to determine the winner of two fencers with the same number of victories.

Beat An attack on the blade, with the intent of opening up the opponent's defence.

Bind A *prise-de-fer*, a taking of the opponent's blade from either the high to low line, or low to high.

Breaking ground Any movement that will take you out of distance of your opponent.

Broken time The loss of one period of fencing time.

Cadence The rhythm of movements during a fencing phrase.

Ceding parries To give way to the attack by a withdrawal of the parry.

Central guard A guard position that does not cover any one line.

Change beat A beat on the opposite side of your opponent's blade.

Change of engagement A taking of the opponent's blade from one line to another.

Circular parry A circular movement of the blade taking your opponent's blade from one line to another, either clockwise or anti-clockwise; the same as a counter-parry.

Close quarters When fencers are too close to use their weapons properly, but without body contact.

Compound attacks Any attack that consists of more than one blade action.

Compound preparation of attack Two preparations executed simultaneously.

Compound *prise-de-fer* Two *prises-de-fer* taken successively, without loss of blade.

Compound riposte A riposte of more than one blade action.

Contraction parries Circular parries on a straight arm in the wrong line.

Coquille The bell shaped guard on the foil and *épée*.

93

Corps-à-corps   When the bodies of both fencers are in contact.

Coulé   Can be either an attack on the blade or a taking of the blade.

Counter-attack   An offensive action against the opponent's attack or preparation.

Counter action parries   Circular parries taken the wrong way.

Counter-disengage   To deceive the opponent's change of engagement either clockwise or anti-clockwise, avoiding any blade contact.

Counter-offensive actions   The Stop-Hit (q.v.) and Time-Hit (q.v.).

Counter-parries   Parries that describe a circular movement of the blade bringing the attacker's blade back into the line that it started from; the same as circular parries.

Counter-riposte   An offensive movement which follows a successful parry of a riposte. It can be delivered by either the attacker or defender; it can be simple or compound.

Counter-time   Drawing the opponent's stop-hit or time-hit, parrying it and riposting from it.

Coupé   The cut-over. The only attack which passes over the opponent's blade, to end in the line opposite to that of the engagement.

Coupé-coupé   Two cut-overs.

Coupé-dessous   A cut-over, followed by disengagement into the low line, most often finishing in *octave*.

Covered   One cannot be hit in the covered line by a straight-thrust.

Croisé   A *prise-de-fer*, takes the blade from the high line to the low line, or vice versa.

Cut   To hit with either the front or back edge of the blade, only allowed at sabre.

Cut-over   The *coupé*.

Cutting the line   Taking a circular parry to the opposite line to normal.

Delayed   To lose a period of fencing time.

Deception   To deceive your opponent's blade actions.

Dérobement   The evasion of the opponent's attempt to take, or attack the blade.

Detachment   To take the blade away from the opponent's.

Développement   The technical name for the lunge.

Disengagement   The passing of the blade from the line of the engagement into the opposite line. One of the four simple attacks.

Doublé   A feint of a disengagement, followed by a counter-disengagement.

Double preparation of attack   Two preparations of attack performed consecutively.

Double *prise-de-fer*   Two *prises-de-fer*, with loss of contact in the middle.

En finale   The last action of the attack.

En marchant   An attack combined with a step forward.

Engagement   When both blades are in contact.

Enveloppement   A taking of the blade which describes a circle with both blades in contact bringing them back to the original line of engagement.

Epée   The largest and heaviest of the three weapons.

False attack   An attack not intended to hit.

Feint   A movement of the blade intending to draw a reaction.

Feint-in-time   A compound stop-hit against the fencer using counter time.

Fencing measure   The practical distance between two fencers.

Fencing time   The time taken to execute a movement of blade, body or foot.

Finger play   The use of the fingers to manipulate the sword.

Flèche   The action of the legs permitting the fencer to reach the opponent by running.

Foible The top half of the blade.

Foil The smallest of the three weapons.

Forte The bottom half of the blade.

Froissement A sharp forward and downward grazing action.

Gaining ground To move forward, advance.

Grip The way that the sword is held; the handle.

Guard The bell-shaped metal in front of the grip, to protect the fingers.

High lines The two guard positions for the top half of the body, i.e., *sixte* and *quarte*.

Hit To score a hit, either with the point or edge, depending on which weapon you are using.

Immediate Any movement made without a pause.

Impetinata To strike the ground with the front foot, immediately before a lunge.

Indirect Any attack or riposte from one line to another.

Inside lines *Quarte* and *septime*.

Judges Four people used in classic fencing to help award hits.

Lines Areas corresponding to the fencing positions.

Low lines The two guard positions for the lower half of the body, i.e., *septime* and *octave*.

Lunge The classical leg action enabling the fencer to reach the target.

Manipulators The fingers and thumb of the hand holding the sword.

Martingale The leather strap that helps to retain the foil in the hand. Replaced by the body-wire of the electric foil.

Metallic jacket The electric jacket that is the target.

Metallic piste The limited fencing area used for competitions.

Molinello A circular cut at head or chest, passing through the *prime* position. (At sabre only.)

On guard or **en garde** The position from which a fencer can guard himself prior to actions either offensive or defensive.

Outside lines *Sixte* and *octave*.

Orthopaedic A colloquial term applied to moulded handles.

Parry A defensive action with the sword deflecting an attack.

Passé feint A feint not followed by an attack.

Plastron A half jacket worn under the main jacket to give extra protection against the opposing weapon.

Pommel The weighted metal end of the handle which holds the weapon together and balances it.

Pool System by which fencers compete against each other in an organised way.

Preparation of attack A blade, body or foot action which opens the way for an attack.

President The umpire in a fencing bout.

Pressure A preparation of attack made by pressing the opponent's blade out of line.

Principle of defence The opposition of *forte* and *foible*.

Prise de fer A taking of the blade.

Pronation When the fingers of the sword hand are directed downwards.

Rassemblement A recovery backwards to the *en garde* position.

Redoublement A renewal of attack or riposte, comprising one or more blade movements.

Remise A renewal of attack, made in the same line of the parry.

Renewals of attack   The *remise, redoublement* and *reprise.*

Reprise   A renewal of attack preceded by a recovery to guard forwards or backwards.

Riposte   The offensive action after a successful parry.

Reverse beat   A beat on the reverse side of the opponent's blade.

Retire   To step backwards, to give ground.

Sabre   The cutting and thrusting weapon.

St George's parry   Sabre *quinte.*

Salute   A blade action of respect to the opponent.

Second intention   A premeditated action to deal with a provoked action.

Semicircular parry   A parry describing a half-circle from high to low, or low to high.

Simple attack   One blade action, direct or indirect.

Simultaneous actions   When both fencers attack together.

Sitting down   The bending of the knees in the on-guard position.

Stance   The position of the feet and body in the on-guard position.

Stop-hit   A counter-offensive action. To be valid must land before the attacker's final movement.

Stop-hit in counter-time   A stop-hit on the opponent's stop-hit.

Straight thrust   A direct and simplest form of attack.

Successive parries   Two or more parries following each other.

Supination   When the fingers holding the weapon are pointed upwards.

Taking the blade   A preparation of attack.

Target   The area of the body on which hits can be scored.

Time-hit   A counter-offensive action which anticipates the final line of the attack. One can hit but must not be hit.

Touche   The French word for a hit.

Trompement   A blade action that deceives the opponent's parries.

Two time   That which is executed in two periods of fencing time.

Uncovered   A position where the line of the engagement is not covered.